Ernest L. Norman
Author, philosopher, poet, scientist, director,
moderator of Unarius Science of Life

UNARIUS
UNiversal ARticulate Interdimensional

Understanding of Science

THE

INFINITE

CONTACT

The Infinite Contact

by

Ernest L. Norman

UNARIUS PUBLICATIONS
145 S. Magnolia Avenue
El Cajon, CA 92020

INFINITE CONTACT

Third Edition

ISBN 0-93264-11-X

Unarius Educational Foundation
El Cajon, California 92020

Other Works by Ernest L. Norman

The Infinite Concept of Cosmic Creation
(The Lesson Course, the key to the Unarius science)

The Pulse of Creation Series:

The Voice of Venus	Vol. 1
The Voice of Eros	Vol. 2
The Voice of Hermes	Vol. 3
The Voice of Orion	Vol. 4
The Voice of Muse	Vol. 5

Infinite Perspectus

Tempus Procedium

Tempus Invictus

Tempus Interludium Vol. I
Of Atoms and Astronauts (Solar Mechanics)

Tempus Interludium Vol. II

Cosmic Continuum

The Elysium (Parables)

The Anthenium

The Truth About Mars

The True Life of Jesus

The Story of the Little Red Box
(By Unarius' Students & E. L. Norman)

Bridge to Heaven
(The Revelations of Ruth Norman, by Ruth Norman)

"Do not worship as does the heathen on street corners nor in public places, neither in the synagogues, nor in the temples, but retire into thine own secret closet and seek out the Father which is Within, that He may reward ye openly."

TABLE OF CONTENTS

PREFACE

Dear Student:

In presenting to you the first of this series of lectures called "The Infinite Contact", and as that familiar cliché says, we do so with mixed emotions, we can therefore be pardoned for a certain amount of justifiable pride; for this presentation represents part of the fruit of attainment which is now being borne as an expression of the principles in these teachings.

To Ruth then, again goes a full measure of recognition in her attainment; also to Helen Moore, a very capable typist who is now finding her expression in these principles. Through various typing and proofreading processes, these two dedicatees have found an expressive companionship which is so necessary before the script reaches the press.*

A word of mention should also be given of the actual transmissions of the texts; that here again, Principle is justified, for these (and all other) transmissions are so delivered in an almost perfect form and require no editing. Sentence structure, composition and words are intact and no material is discarded or rewritten; and incidentally, which comes from a mind which is, comparatively speaking, unlettered so far as the considerations of a formal education are concerned. As consciousness, it retains its equivalent amount of perfection and without such imperialistic dogmas as are always associated with educational protocol. It would be of interest to note that this channel, at a very tender age, was expressing these same mental capabilities even years before he attended his first grade in primary school and was considered an "infant prodigy". Here again is definite proof of reincarnation; the channel merely maintained more or less of a continuity between various past lives—wherein he was highly educated—into his first childhood years of this present life. This is true in all cases where certain precocities are expressed by children.

As for the lectures, they will be presented in no particular order or sequence, for the subject matter is extremely broad. However, each one will strike a decisive blow in your cause for freedom and, with your earnest cooperation and participation, will eventually spring the lock on your prison door—a prison which has held you captive to this earth for many thousands of years.

It might be well to point out that such subject matter which relates more directly to the material world, has been drawn from various existing documentaries and statistics and can be relied upon as accurate. As for the more advanced philosophical and scientific context, much of this material will be verified in future generations of mankind who will live on this earth. Science is already probing into this unknown —a vast macrocosm of countless galaxies and their more countless suns, many with planetary systems where various kinds and races of mankind are living and were living, billions of years before any man appeared upon the earth.

In many of these distant worlds, people are living according to the higher principles explained in these texts. As Jesus said, "Ye must approach the Father as little children." And, as the Father is the Infinite—the sum total of all things visible and invisible—so we must approach this vast Infinity without strong convictions or denials, because "we cannot understand, or accept", for such mental attitudes are extremely inhibitive in nature and will keep us from making a justifiable progression into the future.

It should be remembered that as this Truth is transcribed into the printed word, there also comes with it a great Blessing: for as these texts are so borne out of the Powerhouse of the Infinite Mind, so do they contain a certain Transcending Power—a healing Ray which will, in proportion to your receptiveness, materially aid you in overcoming various obstructions which are presently with you. This Transcendent Power is sometimes physically felt by different students and may cause a mild or violent perspiration as the body is cleansed of inferior elements and its vibrating rate readjusted. Or, this Power may sometimes cause the reader to become strangely drowsy—an almost trance-like condition wherein the conscious mind is temporarily suspended from its usual negative, reciprocating, wave-train oscillation. In any case, however, or in what other appearances this Power may be felt or even if you do not physically feel this Power, *it is with you nevertheless*, and its beneficent effect will be apparent immediately, as it can cleanse, heal and purify all conditions.

There are no magic formulas necessary; only sincere and dedicated purpose in attaining wisdom which will give you spiritual freedom and solvency from the material way of life.

It must be considered that all systems of life, whether they are social, political, governmental or religious have that certain element of dogma. This is especially true with religion. For any religion exists only by application of a very strong dogmatic influence which permeates into every corner of life of the adherent; and all such adherents are thus morally intimidated, directly or indirectly, by this dogmatic influence. In this dogma, all religions therefore stipulate to their adherents complete moral and spiritual subjugation. The hierarchy of the church or temple can, in this subjugation, render any such judgments which will make the adherent conduct himself ac-

3

cordingly. This is a form of slavery perhaps far more abject and subversive than any usually associated physical forms, as this mental subjugation robs the adherent of his integrity, his individuality; it stifles any progressive action and forfeits his inalienable right to determine good from evil. For even in his daily experiences the adherent is pressurized into false attitudes and concepts by this dogmatic subjugation.

It therefore remains with every progressively minded individual as an unalterable fact, that if he wishes to assume and maintain progressive evolutions, he must free himself from all such dogmatic dispensations. This can be done more easily when we can assume that this individual so concerned has had a certain amount of several preconditioning elements. He can say, in a sense, he is completely fed up clear to his ears with all of the turmoil, strife, wars and other such kindred and associated reflexes such as lust, greed, envy, selfishness, fears—all of which are characteristically reactionary and animal-like in nature. The individual must also be spiritually aware; in other words, in the in-between lives or the various psychisms with which he has been consciously or subconsciously attuned, in a higher and more spiritual way of life.

This, then, is the point where he enters into his personal millennium—a long period wherein comparisons between the new and the old life are entered into; new evaluations are made. Many other things too, enter into this reconstructive process, for this person is literally tearing down his old self and along with it, his old worlds; he retains memory of them only as an objective polarized element of knowledge in the new edifice of life which he is constructing. Soon (comparatively speaking), will come the day of emancipation and in the moments of realization he will see, only in memory, his former earth worlds;

4

however, he will remember them vaguely just as he now does his childhood days.

About him will be his new life; a new world constructed from the very Radiant Energy of the Infinite Source. He will mingle with others who have likewise attained their emancipation. His mind will be conscious of many things simultaneously and yet they will not carry any stigma of emotion for he will feel secure in his position—a spiritual being; one not subjected to the old carnal dogmas of the past.

These and many other things will form his new spiritual life, new only in a sense of comparisons in time; for he may have been many countless thousands of years in this attainment since he made his first resolution and dedication; yet even here in this new spiritual world he is looking forward toward new horizons. He sees in the future an even greater purpose, an even greater attainment; for such is the Way of life to all who tread this evolutionary pathway. For as the crest of each hill is attained, there is always a new and ever-widening horizon just ahead.

So then, dear student, lend purpose to your life; justify the reason for your creation and justify your belief in yourself. The acquisition of new wisdom always fulfills and justifies and each new acquirement of wisdom will replace many of your former acquisitions which were really only a new and different way to visualize the Infinite.

"Sufficient unto each day, the evil thereof", for the evil of each day is in its dogmatic implications—the way in which this dogma binds the rhetorical mind to the earth.

To your future then, dear student. May you find the strength to liberate yourself to become a free and independent thinker; one who can rationally integrate the ingredients of logic and wisdom into each day spent upon this pathway. Let night find you not in some perdition, a hell-hole filled with the apparitions

5

of past dogmas and creeds but let night instead, find you with your Heavens filled with starry Lights of future attainments. The luminous radiance of your new knowledge will, like a full moon, make of this night a fairy landscape and there you will rest in peace until the dawn of a new day.

*Mention should be given to Dorothy Ellerman who serves most selflessly in her clerical and proofing efforts; thoroughly dedicated.

NOTE:

The Creative Abstract

In giving a discourse, as is so done by the Channel of Unarius, it is much more than merely putting thoughts into words. It must be the creation of a great Vortex of energy wherein are compounded in abstract form, all pertinent and relative information contained in the word-form discussion. The reader then automatically "tunes in" while reading, to the vortex—the abstract information. This, in turn, polarizes various constituents and configurations in the psychic consciousness of the individual and he has truly learned the subject matter.

This is quite different than the commonly understood learning which is normally associated with healing. As there is no vortex which would give the reader a polarization in these many infinite abstractions, we must therefore subconsciously create wave train patterns which are called memory.

Subconscious wave train patterns never impart the true meaning or learning to the individual because rapport has not been attained with all psychic centers and with the Cell of the Infinite called the Superconscious.

True learning takes place only when this rapport has been attained; not only subconsciously but as a polarizing intelligence which helps re-create the Higher Spiritual Self.

CHAPTER 1

The Great Enigma — Religion

Now that the Christmas season is upon us and that inasmuch as we are surrounded with these demonstrative effusions, it might be well to ponder upon what is perhaps the most enigmatical of all lives lived—the life of Jesus. For while it truly can be said that in His own way He gave a certain measure of Truth, far greater than any other person who has lived in present-day historical configurations, yet the eight hundred million or so persons who have accepted Christianity, prima facia, just as countless other millions in the past, and who have accepted all the apparent contradictions, travesties, yes, even the great tragedy of this religion as it has been and is currently being expressed—for these masses to adhere to the cross—they are only substituting new configurations for old.

The cross, the flame or the burning orb of the sun are but re-adaptations of old protocols, and fanfares, and various impedimenta which are classically associated with various paganistic religions; for in his acceptance, the Christian has either set aside or refused to use the like of either historical knowledge or pure reason and logic, and is still strongly motivated with the dire need to relieve psychic pressures from guilt complexes with the same age-old mental automation —the escape mechanism—which reaches its greatest and most predominant proportion of expression in the various collective religions of the world.

In his endeavor to escape from reality, the Christian is not so concerned in the various enigmas of his religion. How could such a religion, which was purported or supposed to give man spiritual emancipation but which was founded upon mob violence and murder give this freedom? And could such a simple direct approach to life as was taught by Jesus, be supported amid the garish trappings, the altar robes, deistic configurations, ceremonies and other symbolic protocol associated not only with Christianity but any other religion? For while this man, Jesus, taught Truth simply, sitting by the wayside, the so-called dispensers of this Truth have found a way to purvey it for fancy prices, amid the settings of barbaric splendor.

The life of Jesus, itself, needs much of the light of compromise and understanding if we are to garner the few pearls of wisdom remaining in the testaments; for here again is a great enigma—a paradox if you please—that seems to defy constructive analysis and mandates either a blind acceptance, or complete rejection.

Could it be that He was no more than an ordinary man; or could a person who was thus so minded as He, and could perform thousands of miracles be so limited in future prognostications; could He not look into the future and see the countless millions who would be trapped in this same pit of clay which had been their common lot with other religions in past lives? Could He not see the millions who would die fighting for His name in some great religious war, or those millions who would die as martyrs—a gesture of revenge to purge His name of some fancied sin?

Yes, there is all this and much more which He could have seen—even to the future far beyond our time; for even now, as the Christmas season is again bringing forth its symbolisms and depictions of the past, it is again predicting the same future for the many millions who will yet live as Christians.

CHAPTER 2

The Duality of Jesus

Any material man is vitally concerned with various portions of his anatomy; the loss of any of its members is a tragedy or dire catastrophe. The man philosophically inclined is not so concerned but knows he can live without fingers or toes or even arms or legs; yes, he knows he can live—even after death.

Yes, the people of the Holy Land who saw the man, Jesus, saw only one small nether part of a great spiritual anatomy, the more highly developed Superconscious Self of a Spiritual entity which was functioning creatively in many directions simultaneously. It, (the Superconscious Self), was not personally conscious of, but was philosophically aware of the embodiment of Jesus and related, or expressed itself, through Him only in propitious moments, wherein the Self of Jesus became more directly related to this Higher Self. Under these more favorable conditions, the Higher Self then functioned and the miracles were performed. However, it must be remembered that this Higher Self always functioned with logic and reason far above the level commonly ascribed to lower physical man and therefore was not affected by the emotional content of reactionary experiences.

This Higher Self could then concern Itself, through Jesus, with various expressions as miracles or personal realizations—vindications of understanding of higher principles to those few thousands who had at that time so preconditioned themselves, had prepared for, and had met the necessary requirements in the spiritual worlds and, in the earth life realizations, were thus enabled through Jesus to turn their faces toward this Higher Spiritual entity and, in the directive flow of constructive energies, receive their personal miracle or realization.

This Higher Self knew and realized much more so than did the man Jesus, of demonstrating in a time, or a material world environment; that inversely, the greater the positive polarity of time, the greater the negative polarity which would tend to equalize or neutralize such great spiritual expurgations and which would completely deviate any individual from his natural evolutionary pathway. For the Higher Self knew that this negative polarity so expressed, has powerful and dominant sub-astral agencies and would seize this participle of expressed Truth and from it reconstruct their own pagan dispensations so that it would be torn apart and dismembered and its various parts would be tossed to the members of the hierarchies in the various factional religions; and there, like grizzly trophies from some great war, would be hung upon their cross for the masses to kneel before and pay humble homage—to lay upon the altar the supreme sacrifice, their God-given birthright of the personal relative expression to the Infinite; and for a time, being like moles burrowing beneath the ground, their purpose would be waylaid by these floods of religious negation; yet, find the Light they must; their blind and almost unopened eyes longed for the Light; their bodies longed for the warmth of new understanding.

And so, as of today, the bells of many Christian lands peal forth a complex sound and, like the links in a chain, each one forged in the manner of its own destiny; so do these sounds, like chains, bind the multitudes who hear them. Yes, bound indeed they are—not to the present but to the past; for these sounds of bells are stronger indeed than any chains forged from steel and their clanking is reminiscent of the dungeons wherein countless thousands died for the Christ and with a prayer to Christ on their lips; theirs a meaningless death shared only with a meaningless purpose. Yes, as of today, though the dungeons are gone, all men are no less confined, for in believing what they hear is the true promise of the future, they have condemned themselves and, for a time at least, their death warrants must be executed.

For no man hears the true sounding bell until that day and time when from somewhere deep within himself he hears the clarion call of the Infinite and, upon the first steps of logic and reason, he will begin the long-drawn-out process of spiritual emancipation from the dross, mud, slime and ooze of the material world from whence he sprang. For even as he so began, he was a part of the whole, and in living and realizing the wholeness of all things, lived many strange ways, fought many battles and died in devious manners, always to be born again from the shambles and wreckage of his past; and from this past, pick up his new armor and sword and fight his way again to a vainglorious end.

Now, poised for the first time upon the steps of reason and logic, he can turn and look back into the past; nor will be turned to a pillar of salt for so looking, for his footing is firm and he falls not, nor can the black past reach out with tentacled hands to grasp and hold him for he is shielded with a new armor—not made with the fabrications of his past—but with a garment woven with the strands of Truth, Light and luminous in its virtues, transforming him from a mundane materialistic creature into an ethereal entity; yet no will-o'-the-wisp but strong and powerful in the virtue of knowledge; with a new sword, shield and buckler made from the elements of wisdom and purpose. And in the purpose of all things, he will wage a new war—not one like any of the past but a war against the minions of the underworld, the swarming, vampire-like bats of hatred, greed and malice, the vultures of hypocrisy, the wolves of intolerance and the dragons of selfishness—all will fall beneath his flaming sword.

Such is the way of life, that through the very nature of vileness and evil, man is forced to seek good and always does he find this good, even in the very bowels of iniquity.

Yes, indeed, the life of Jesus presented a good many strange and inexplicable contrasts: one moment the Superman who healed lepers or raised the dead. Was this the same man who knelt in tearful supplication in the last hours in Gethsemane? Yes, even in crying out in agony upon the cross, was this the same man of whom the shortest verse was written in the testaments and was so quoted in two words, "Jesus wept." (Book of John). A strange contrast, of a weak emotional human or a towering pillar of spiritual Light and power, all fully justified and understandable when the hidden principle is revealed.

For this, our earth, is a primitive world where life lives to kill or to be killed; to survive by the fang and claw or so live to die by them and, as each man is born and in thus being born, like all earth things is condemned to death. All things begin to decay even as they begin to grow and the Higher Beings of which Jesus was one, in knowing of these things—how brave these Souls are to venture into these astral worlds—for such they are; yet even in their venture they are not unwise but do so in a manner and way which is acceptable to the world and which supports the reason for the venture.

And so the effigy is created; perhaps an ordinary man, born of the womb and swaddled in the clothes of the nursery yet lives to be visited by the Higher

14

Self. And while these visitations are always accompanied by symbolical manifestations, there is the time in between when the body must live as the earthman does and in this living finds the earth as others do, always awaiting the transcendent moment when the Visitor arrives.

So look not upon the man Jesus as your Savior but live only for the things which saved Him also. Understand the Jesus as He is and was two thousand years ago—a Super Being who found part of His continuity in Divine expression through the body of an earthman.

Understand immaculate conception for what it really is: impregnation of consciousness from the Infinite Mind through the polarization of self in conscious living. To live in the future world means complete transformation of self with the Divine Alchemy of the Infinite Mind. It means subtraction of the old material elements which were once necessary in the earthly life and, in knowing of these and many other things and in their practice and usage, you, too, may become a Super Being to find one common form of expression in some material world as an earthman —but with Infinite purpose and realization; and in that day you will have found your new Christmas— the rightful birthplace of your own personal Savior.

CHAPTER 3

Origin of Christianity

Look not therefore in the garish tinseled trappings of the Christmas season for the true meaning of Christmas, for this is indeed the greatest of all symbologies expressed by the millions of Christian adherents. Yes, and even as of this time and place, such large and small symbologies have replaced logic and reason and, enigmatically, even the origin of these symbologies is lost or unknown to the Christian constituents.

How many Christians know that their gaily tinseled tree was once the symbolic expression of a certain spiritual configuration worshiped by the Druids a thousand or more years ago; that at the time of the winter solstice, the week beginning on the 21st of December, votive offerings would be given to this spirit in the form of a virgin maiden whose lifeless body was hung upon the tree? How many Christians know that one of the dominant spiritual characterizations of their religion, one called Jehovah, is an old pagan god erected in pre-Babylonian days for various purposes associated with the religion of that time and place, including human sacrifice; and that this pagan god Jehovah was brought out of Babylonia by Father Abraham and perpetuated to the Christians through the Old Testament? How many Christians know that by and large all ceremonies and observan-

16

ces, such as the resurrection, have their counterparts in ancient pagan or heathen religions? Yes, even the resurrection is depicted on the temple walls of Ancient Egypt; Osiris, the godfather and judge, with Horus his one and only Son as Intercessor or Savior; Horus begotten of Isis, mother of Earth, through immaculate conception.

These and many other ancient deistic concepts born and fostered in age-old and almost forgotten civilizations, now again live in Christianity, just as they have lived from the time of Paul and Peter. For even the birth of Jesus and the manner of His birth is one which was borrowed by Paul in the beginning of the Christian Church. It is well known historically, that when Paul began this Christian Church in Ancient Greece, he had to proselyte converts from at least two strong and well-known religions. One of these was Mithraism, a degenerate and pagan form of a religion founded, partially at least, upon Zoroasterianism a thousand years before that time in northwest Persia, by a man known as Zoroaster (or Zarathustra).

Facts and figures of this man's life, while partly legendary, are still part of the religion of about 100,000 Parsees in Western India. Zoroaster who later became known as Mithras, the god of light or the sun, was born of immaculate conception in a shepherd's hut or manger, the event being witnessed by shepherds who had come down from a nearby hillside. Overhead was a huge star. This was Ahura-Mazda, (the Father of all, the counterpart of Jehovah in this province). Later three soothsayers came from a nearby town to take the young mother back to the palace, as she was of royal birth. It is quite obvious that Paul borrowed this story to dress up his otherwise drab religion.

Actually Jesus was born in the women's quarters of the temple. All temples in Ancient Chaldea and Babylonia were constructed with a women's quarters, just as was King Solomon's temple in Jerusalem;

17

their sole purpose being that of a maternity ward for the young maidens who had come to the temple to be prepared for marriage. This is an ancient custom of fertility (and still practiced in some countries), which had been brought out of Ancient Chaldea by Father Abraham and was still a strong part of the Jewish religion at the time of Jesus.

When a young girl entered puberty, she went to the temple and there the reigning deity or god would per-forate the hymen. This was of course done in proxy by a priest. The purpose among other things was to remove the stigma of shame from sex in her married life and to insure a large family, preferably males, all of whom would be endowed with more wisdom and god-like qualities. Occasionally the maiden became pregnant in the process; then in her last months of pregnancy she would be confined in the women's quarters of the temple until delivery, when at that time an older man would be given to her as husband. This was but a saving grace measure which would enable the young lady to reenter her social life with-out shame.

The child in question, if a male, was raised as a priest, the female babies usually disappearing in obscure ways. While this fertility custom may at first seem very shocking upon its revelation, yet it was, to those who observed and practiced it, a very necessary and vital part of their religion and was quite sacred in nature. The Saint James Bible with the concordance has a map of the temple of Jerusalem which shows the location of the women's quarters.

As a matter of fact, there is little beyond certain portions of this literal translation which refers to the life of Jesus in the fabric of Christianity which cannot be considered as readapted forms of legendary or real pagan beliefs and their associated protocols. Even the four synoptic gospels were not written by those persons whose names they bear, but were actually ordered so written by Paul; the actual writings being done by two of his priests, Clostideous and Ireneous. No doubt he was displeased with the first and each succeeding version, thus accounting for the four.

However, Paul may or may not be accused of all the chicanery which entered into the formation of the new church, for much of the present-day Christian observances and protocols were part of that Mithraic cult from which the new church gained so many of its converts and it is easy to see how these various beliefs and observances were merged into the new church.

While Paul, who was actually Saul of Tarsus, half Roman half Jew, former tentmaker and persecutor of the Nazarenes, could be considered in this respect, a charlatan and a fraud who was obsessed and driven by a strong guilt complex, yet perhaps he was not responsible for such later mergings and readaptations of various Mithraic forms.

As Mithraism was compounded from both the ancient Zoroasterianism and the even more ancient Egyptian Osirianism, many such classical examples reappear in various portions of the Christian Bible. Zoroaster prophesied the day of doom when Ahura-Mazda would sweep the earth with fire which would flow like milk and destroy all the wicked; and after a cooling-off period, or millennium, the good souls would then be resurrected in new bodies to reinhabit the new earth, which had been thus cleansed and purified from evil and want. This too, has an Osirian counterpart formed in the resurrection and intercession by Horus. For Horus was the exact counterpart of Mithras and, as Sons of God through immaculate conception and thus endowed with godlike propensities, became the Saviors of mankind.

How easily did Jesus reoccupy this same niche in the new Christianity. This however, is only a small part of the many analogies found in Mithraism and Christianity. In Mithraism there was the winter solstice, the 25th of December to the 1st, a period of feasting, rejoicing and gift giving, followed by forty days of various festive spring occasions.

These various customs and observances later found their readapted forms as the Christian Epiphany in "lent", the 25th actually becoming the fictitious birthday of Jesus. Other Christmas observances and readaptations drawn from Mithraism include the resurrection as in ancient Osirianism. Osiris slew the black bull, the personification of all evil, which later became the Christian devil. After slaying the bull, Osiris, mortally wounded, retired and on the third day, being immortal, arose. Even the devil is also the Zoroastrian counterpart, or Ahriman. Thus began the Christian Church, and from the roots of ancient pagan beliefs, rituals, observances and customs sprang the first trunk of the Christian Church which was later to be split by the forces of dissention; one part to form the Greek orthodox, the other the Roman Catholic. Yes, even the Roman Peter, the supposed founder of that great church, is the former Mithraic Petra, or the rock; the rock which formed the tomb for the original Mithraic version of the resurrection.

CHAPTER 4

Background of Christianity

It might be conceded that the context of the fore-going paragraphs is indeed startling or even shocking to some of those who read them. Indeed it might even appear that the author is atheistic and attempting to destroy Christianity, and perhaps other religions of the world. Therefore, to soften such shocks or to justify to the reader, not in defense for no defense is needed in the presentation as this material was drawn from various existing histories, these are facts which may be a part of either private or public libraries. Indeed the reader may find that the author has presented this historical background of Christianity very briefly and that further studies along these lines would not only clarify and enlarge the foregoing contents but would add other similar parallels to this background of Christianity.

For instance, in Mithraism before it became merged into Christianity, the custom of baptism was a ritual of purification wherein the subject being so baptized was completely immersed in pure cow urine. Could this be the same baptismal, the same symbol of purification, the washing away of sins etc., which is dramatically described in the New Testament when John baptized Jesus in the river Jordan; and if baptism is for purification, why then did the "only begotten Son of God" need purifying?

21

The places of Mithraic worship which were among the tall forest trees or sometimes in caves or grottos, reformed themselves in Christian places of worship as the tall, columned or pillared church, or cathedral edifices with the arched grotto-like niches at the ends which housed the altars. The liturgy of Christianity contains many other parallels with not only Mithraism but in many other pagan or deistic religions of the world, both modern and ancient.

So far as the philosophical teachings of Christianity are concerned (and as is contained in the Bible), it is indeed a strange and extremely complex matrix of symbologies, ideologies, superstitions, etc., combined with some rather questionable historical data. Nor can the reader take refuge in attempting to justify his past understandings by referring to the Dead Sea Scrolls, for these scrolls only substantiate, to some degree, this historical content of the Old Testament. Such verifications, however, must not be confused with the supernatural ideologies which are contained within these texts, and that by and large and from any historical source whatsoever, the Jehovah of the Old Testament is and always will remain a pagan god. Any conduct individually or collectively which implies moral or religious intercourse in the belief of this Jehovah is therefore paganistic; for this Jehovah was completely disproved by Jesus.

Christianity also contains other strange paradoxes which, to the rational thinker, would be apparent immediately. For instance, Jesus taught that all men were equal in the sight of God; therefore every man, woman and child on the face of the earth was a child of this God, irrespective of race, color or creed and that so far as God was concerned, all had the same rights and considerations. All were quite worthy of any help which could be given them; this, Jesus demonstrated by healing and teaching to all, regardless of whether they were Jew, Pharisee, Arab or slave.

However, the modern church liturgy believes that according to a certain prophecy in Revelations, "Only 144,000 people will be saved to inhabit the new city of Jerusalem." What then about the countless billions of people who have swarmed upon the face of this earth, most of whom have not known about Jesus or this so-called Christian way to salvation?

With the destruction of these people and on the judgment day, as is believed by the Christian, God would therefore defeat his own plan and purpose of salvation. For, if and when such a plan was conceived by the Almighty, He would not have needed to have created the earth nor all of the races of mankind. He could have saved Himself all this bother, time and work by taking enough mud and ribs and making Himself 144,000 people and putting them in His new city and keeping them there, much like a boy keeps a bunch of pet rabbits.

Of course this is ridiculous and asinine and no person with a grain of intelligence would believe in this malarkey which has been handed down from generation to generation, race to race, era to era and epoch to epoch by these old witch doctors who have, through successive evolutions, reappeared from time to time and donned the robes of various temples and churches to again purvey this religious hypocrisy.

To intimidate and coerce through fear and other reactive elements in the subconscious, to take advantage of every emotional weakness in their fellowman —this they have done in the past and this they are doing in the present and will continue to do in the future so long as there are those who will support them by going to their temples and churches with their generosity which is one of the more godlike attributes each man possesses.

No, indeed, the author is not attempting to destroy Christianity or any other religion; he knows how essential such systems are in the first progressive steps of evolution and which are man's first acknowledgment of the great mysterious creative forces. He knows that as every man started as a small cell or entity of consciousness which began to reappear or reincarnate in cyclic movements from life to life, that through frequency relationship this entity of consciousness gathered about it and wove together other entities which were harmonically attuned to it. Thus begins each man as he has always begun and, as he starts this evolutionary pathway, so will he find this pathway threading its way among the things with which he is familiar and which were either partly or wholly responsible for this regenerative process stemming from the Infinite Source.

For, as this Infinite Source is Infinite and that this Infinity is all things visible and invisible, known and unknown, so likewise must this Infinity be maintained by an infinite number of finite forms. Man therefore becomes the collective agency of this infinite number of forms, which he does by living from life to life through the doorway of experience, thus becoming another one of the ultimate achievements of this regenerative process of the Infinite Mind.

For as each man becomes godlike in nature and expression, so must he too, just as does this Infinite Mind, know of all things; and, in the knowing of these things, becomes a participating agent or element, not as a reactionary force in a negative way, but as a positive polarity which supplies a spiritual life, libido or drive, a constructive purpose, and again a reliving of consciousness with the Infinite. Until such time therefore, that any particular individual can conceive or realize these creative principles, he must therefore support his purpose of life, his evolution and all of the things with which he is so concerned at any given time or moment, with all of the elements of the world in which he lives, for these too are but products of his evolution.

As he was before, so he is, and thus he goes from day to day, from life to life and in each day, or each life, he adds or subtracts but very little, for the unknown is a great and terrible monster, more to be feared than the evils of his present moment. Not until he realizes the constructive interplay of the Infinite Mind does he begin to Light his own pathway; the gloomy shadows will disappear, and there will be no unknown monsters. He will, in this self-realization, realize that new dimensions of consciousness are not attained by continuing to ascribe to local social systems and religions, for in these things he listens and sees only with the ears and eyes of other people.

Self-realization is realization of the Infinite Mind, and the position of self as a constructive participating element of consciousness with this Infinite. How useless then is anything, save that it serves a purpose, and that having served its purpose must pass on. How well it is for us to realize its purpose and to witness its passing in the realization of new purposes, for this indeed is progressive evolution—the dynamics of the Infinite Mind in the never-ending, never-ceasing, re-creative process of thought, form and consciousness. "Seek ye first the kingdom of heaven, which is within, and all things shall be added unto thee."

CHAPTER 5

Man's Mind — An Integrator

How well it is to think of these and many other things which have always been associated with religion, such as it may have been in any time or place for these religions, large or small, serve only a primitive man in his first steps toward understanding the Infinite and of the principle and purpose of the Infinite. The great masses of humanity who come and go like surging tides upon the face of this planet, thus have, and are so currently expressing their first yearning to understand. In their religion they have manifest their first acknowledgment and, having taken these first steps, so must pass on to take the next and higher steps.

Too, those who are thus mindful and conscious of the beginning of the evolutionary pathway into the Higher Realms and of their progressive evolution, and who must find a more creative and expressive continuity in the higher principles of life, should know within their own reason that they cannot express and participate in a higher evolutionary conjunction with the Infinite Mind without realizing this one obvious fact: that such journeys into the Higher Realms are not possible when a person is so weighed down with the dogmas and creeds of various social and religious systems, for these are but the compounded reactive elements of past lifetime experiences and must be cleansed of their reactive or emotional element through polarization with the Higher Self.

True spiritual emancipation and a conjunctive function with the Infinite Mind begin only with any person who attains such elements of mental function which are not reactionary products of the subconscious mind and its various compounds of past life experience. Conjunction and function with the Infinite begins when the mental prospectus includes all such necessary and active ingredients of life, completely detached from the emotional and reactionary expression which is common to all materialistic persons. Such a lofty and idealistic mind function is indeed difficult to conceive; for such as it is, the mental or surface mind is merely an integrator and not a creative entity, as some suppose.

Until such time therefore that this surface mind can be detached from the subconscious and begin to function more completely with the Higher Self, the materialist must wander back and forth across the face of the earth in many lives and in these lives, serving many Masters; Masters he has served in the past in many ways and forms and he has called them by many names. They have been his king or his emperor and they have assumed many other forms of past masters and mistresses but greatest of all of these has been the priest, whether he was of a church or a temple, or the witch doctor in the hut. For always he has seen with the eyes of these priests, the workings of the great mystical forces and always he has heard the words of these forces through their ears; and so he rests not, neither does he sleep, a nomad, and from dawn to dusk crossing the barren sands of his earth life, then again to lie in the blackened darkness of some astral spirit world until the dawn of a new life.

Yet, as in all nights, there are stars and there may even be a moon so it may be that as this earthman lies in his blackened night, he may look up and see these stars; yes, he may even see the moon and as he sees these heavenly bodies, his night is lighted by their rays, so much so that he will rise up from where he lies and find that long-sought-after hidden pathway that will lead him out of the barren hinterland of his material world. And as he travels on his new-found pathway, a new dawn will find him high upon the hillside where there are running streams, sunlit pathways through forest glades, trees hung with the ripe fruit of fulfillment which will refresh and nourish him on his way.

Haste then, Oh pilgrim, for while the blackness of this material night is ever about thee, yet if thou will lookest, there will be the stars; yes, even the moon and in their Light, truly then thou will findeth the path and thy new day will find thee high upon thy journey into fulfillment.

CHAPTER 6

The Song of Creation

As for the white dove which fluttered down and the speaking of the voice of God, this is an obvious embellishment, a bit of chicanery, if you please, which would so slant these various descriptive depictions with the necessary supernatural aura. As for the voice of God and any such reputed speaking of this voice, this can be considered as such obvious devices, or that those who heard this voice were suffering from a certain neurotic illness, called by modern psychologists, as traumatic hallucinations; for indeed how can God speak with such a voice for God is not a personal being but is the sum and substance of the Infinite.

Nor does He need to speak in any voice or language, for His message is ever and always about us, a voice which speaks in that constant, never-ending resurgent pattern of life; the creative and re-creative forms of all things of which mankind is conscious; yes, and of all things which will be his even beyond eternity. Nor is God's word so contained in any book, for even as the Christian says his Bible is the word of God, he is only giving his strength to a great lie, for no man can understand or know of God through this book.

If he would hear the Voice of God let him listen to the song of creation which is ever about him; let him see, in his daily actions, the form and substance of this Word. And though blind his eyes may be, and deaf are his ears, if he will look and listen long enough, he will see and hear the Word of God reenacted in a thousand ways. And in seeing and hearing this Word, it will become a golden shuttle filled with the gossamer filament of life; and in his daily actions, his will will give this shuttle power to weave for him a new fabric of life, a cloak of Immortality.

Yes, the Word will do all this and much more, for as the Word becomes the stream of life, so does this stream wash away the earthly stains. It will water the arid wastelands of the mind and from these places shall spring the fruits of realization and fulfillment. For the Word comes not as a Voice so minded and mindful of its own pleasures and hates nor does this Voice command. Neither are there things within this Voice which would lend lustful purpose, false desires, or murderous intent.

To those then, who are mindful of their future, that if they would like to live unto the day of self-realization, to the great day of personal emancipation, then trust not this destiny into the hands of others, for these others may also be seeking the same destiny and despite their claims, always remember that God has never given power to one man over another, nor has He relegated or dispensed His various attributes of inspiration, healing, wisdom and solace through either one or a collective group of people or in any religion in which they believe. For such godlike attributes come only to men who have searched and found them from within themselves and, with the finding, lose the need of the material world and pass on into the higher realms of life.

To you, dear reader, look not then in the Bible or in any other so-called holy word for your salvation, your attainment; neither look in any temple or church, for these are but a few of the many ways in which mankind has striven to understand the great

Creative Infinite. And yet these strivings have always resolved themselves into a coexistent state between the lower carnal self, the animal man, and the embodiment of a psychic form which was first conceived in all things in the Infinite Mind, and which must be born again and lived through this animal body; and live there it must, to be reborn again until the day it finds its purpose; and with the finding of Purpose, will come Realization.

Since the days of the beginnings of Christianity, men have lived and died to justify their cause and there are others too, who have lived and died just as have the others; not for this cause but to prove this cause was one of great error and sinister purpose. For, as Christianity was so founded by those who sought to escape the perditions of their own self-made hell, so it is with all those who ascribe to such religious systems. For here they have found a way, seemingly at least to temporarily relieve the pressure of their own guilts; yet never finding an end to this never-ending nightmare, the ghoulish apparitions of lies, hates, lusts, greeds, malices and emotions borne from out the savage past where an eye was taken for an eye, or a tooth for a tooth; yet ever does necessity to relieve this great guilt increase.

And increase it will, until the judgment day when each man judges all thought and action with the Light of Purpose—a Light which shines through the eye of the Infinite Creator. And as each man finds this judgment and seeing it in the Light of Purpose, all things then become as they must be, all part of this great Infinite; and as each man judges, each man becomes wise in the way of all things; yet in the judgment he must judge not save those things which appear as his own. For should he judge another man's sins, then his own sins go unrecognized, and if he finds not his own sins, they must be with him as they always were.

NOTE

Biblical historians and other historical sources believe Jesus was actually born in the temple, His birthday the 2nd of April—His true paternal father was Annanias who appears in the book of Acts as the judge and prosecutor of Paul. There is strong circumstantial evidence to support this belief.

It is well known that Jesus spent many of His boyhood years living in the temple grounds with His foster mother Mary and His foster father, Joseph, a carpenter, whose task it was to keep the temple in repair.

No doubt it was this close contact with the workings of the temple in His boyhood, which later powered a tremendous incentive to overthrow the tyrannical hypocrisy which He witnessed as the daily practice of Rabbinical dispensations. It is also well established that the babe Jesus was not taken to Egypt but instead was taken to Mount Carmel, the area where He spent His first six years among the Essenes, a cult of spiritual intellectuals. Among these people the child Jesus found ample opportunity to learn much wisdom, as well as to reorient the new physical body with the Higher Self. This will easily explain how, at a later time, Jesus was able to confound the priests in the temple.

In line with these and other historical findings, the Rosecrucians have, as part of their historical literature, expressed strong evidence that Jesus did not die on the cross, but a last hour reprieve was granted by Pilate, He being taken down then by His faithful followers and to satisfy the Rabbis, was then placed in the tomb. There with His wonderful recuperative powers, He was healed quickly of His wounds; His followers returned at night and rolled away the stone, Jesus then going into hiding until He appeared publicly to His faithful followers.

CHAPTER 7

The Decadent Age

More than 2,500 years ago, a Greek philosopher was asked how to become wise. He replied, "Know thyself." It is doubtful that this man, wise as he was, knew the full impact of this utterance; and so these words have become the classical understatement of history. For while it is possible, theoretically at least, for an individual to evolve into a state of consciousness which would seemingly encompass all elements and perspectives known to mankind, yet it is inconceivable for any man to know himself in his entirety. Indeed it is, that the very nature of Infinity is constantly adding to the prospectus of every individual, unknown and intangible elements, and the desire to learn of these things creates a libido or drive to satisfy this demand to acquire knowledge of these unknown elements.

While on the positive side, curiosity of the unknown has often led man into his greatest discoveries and achievements, yet the predominant driving force or mainspring of life is fear. Fear is either a product of bygone ages or is carried through the pattern of evolution into our present time; and in more modern times fear is no less, despite modern scientific technology which supposedly eliminates various sources of fear from our daily lives. Indeed, this very technocracy has, by its very affluence of various scientific achievements, increased fear a hundredfold.

Since the dawn of time and the beginning of man's life upon this earth when he first started as a primitive creature, the jungle trails were filled with many dangers. Fear was the coercive force which kept him alive, for the primitive law, "survival of the fittest", demanded that only the strongest bodies, the keenest eyes and ears and the quickest reflexes would survive and breed another generation.

This is the first and most primitive principle by which man has learned to live; a principle made mandate by the Infinite which would enable the lower bestial forms of mankind to evolve to the point where reason and logic would supplant this old carnal law. Yet as of today, no individual indigenous to this planet earth, has arrived at the point of emancipation from coercive fear and the primitive law of survival. It is an inescapable fact, despite various platitudes which he has showered upon himself, that his religion or technocracy has not and will not absolve him from his primitive fear and survival situation.

Science has eliminated many killers of the weaklings. It has also invented new and more terrible methods of mass murder. Through systems of communication, science has shrunk the earth and pushed aside all natural environmental barriers. With each advance in technocracy, created supposedly for the benefit of mankind, it has only increased his fear and made his life more complex; for these very creative forces and efforts in which man has sought to better himself and to raise his standard of living are as a two-edged sword cutting both ways.

Thus the future generations will live to see the destruction of this civilization by the very forces which created it. This may at first appear as a great enigma, but past history will prove the truth of these statements. Babylonia, Egypt, Greece, Rome, Carthage are but a few of the great past civilizations which have thus so perished; and would it be, that for the benefit of humanity mankind at this present time had leadership with foresight and understanding, it could prevent future disintegration of this civilization.

Perhaps it is too late, for the hour has already struck which began the downward fall of this age. The dynamic creative forces which brought it out of the darkened past have passed the point of equilibrium; for as the will and necessity for survival became the creative and driving force, the necessity to waylay fear, anxiety and insecurity and in the creation and achievement, then began to foster a degenerated race of people. A massive horde of humanity began to lead a puppet-like existence through complex social systems, preponderant masses of laws and an ever increasing tempo of life.

Man has now found himself inextricably caught in the web of his own making; a great vortex which is sucking him down into oblivion. You doubt these statements? Then let us look at statistics. More than 29 percent of the American public is suffering from comparatively mild or advanced forms of various mental aberrations and badly in need of corrective therapy. A statement made by J. Edgar Hoover, F.B.I. Chief, in recent articles published by a national news syndicate was that more than 51 percent of all crime committed is by the American youth before the age of twenty-one years. More than 30 percent of all dope addicts are found in this group and, incidentally, figures on crime and dope addiction are staggering. According to Encyclopedia Britannica, juvenile delinquency is rapidly increasing and has more than doubled since 1948, as compared to a 19 percent increase in population; one typical year, 1955-56, a 22 percent increase as compared to a 4 percent increase in population.* Nor do we need to look in these directions for evidence of decadency, for all about us are the telltale signs of moral and spiritual decay; the same destructive trend which obliterated so many past civilizations. Through various fields of entertainment and communication, the American public has literally been drenched in a sewage of drug and sex abuse, lust and murder; radio, motion pictures, television as well as magazines and newspapers, have been the carriers and purveyors of this vile brew, steeped in the black cauldrons of the lowest hells and destined in its manufacture by the lords of the underworlds, to enslave humanity—to destroy the last fiber of moral tissue.

And there are other agents which are aiding and abetting the common destruction of this civilization. The psychic pressures of these times have turned millions to alcoholism and perhaps worst of all in some respects, the cigarette habit as well as drugs.

The dollar cost of smoking is staggering; consumption per capita is 11.5 pounds, costing the American smoker over five billion dollars annually! Of the fire bill of $1,023,190,000 in 1957, 26 percent was caused by matches and smoking. More than 20,000 lose their lives yearly in fires—of these 4,000 die in bed as a result of that last cigarette; 8,000 children die yearly in fires, playing with matches and cigarettes—imitating adults—and numerous others die in fires caused by careless smoking habits; yet these losses are small by comparison to the uncalculated loss of personal health and longevity suffered by the smoker. Only study and research could give you the true picture of what this one nefarious practice has done to the masses of humanity swarming upon the face of this globe.

These and many more important destructive factors have given power to the finger which has already written the prophecy of doom upon the wall. No, it shall not be a nuclear weapon or another war which will destroy man and his civilization; he will destroy himself when he has passed the point of equilibrium wherein the dynamic progressive powers which motivate his progressive evolution no longer function as factors of integration in advancing his position in infinite prospectus.

In passing this point, he outlives the necessity of his being. He is no longer useful either to himself or to the Infinite, for in this pathway of all men, there must always be a constructive balance which outweighs the seemingly destructive or reactionary.

To you who are Truth seekers, be not afraid of the appearances or disappearances of civilizations, or that your world of today is faced with destruction. This has always been so and as it should be, for it is the way of the Infinite Mind to right certain imbalances which have occurred in the selective processes of life as they concern mankind in general.

This is the way the Infinite purges itself, so to speak, of the great negations; to discharge negative static energies which have accumulated through wrong usage and wrong living. And, as the Infinite cleanses itself in this cyclic manner and form, so may you too learn to discharge negative static forces which have accumulated in your dimension of life; static forces which have been called karma and which tie the individual to a wheel-like cyclic repetition of various configurations of experiences which are revolving in the vortexes of these negative static forces.

In our present-day world, much can be seen in the vein of psychic affiliations and that humanity is constantly expressing, in numerous ways, manners and forms, these various psychic affiliations with the past: the ladies who don the garb and raiment of some past life in which they lived in masculine attire as a male, and some of the males of this day who psychically remember themselves as females despite strong outward displays of masculine propensities, admit feminine attributes in many subtle ways; yes, even occasional examples of completely reverting to a female life. Could the screaming masses jumping up and down upon the seats of our modern coliseums be part of the same masses of humanity who screamed and jumped in the time of Nero or in the last days of Pompeii? And could our baseball and football heroes who trample the sod on these fields be the old gladiators who trampled the sand and many times reddened it with their blood in these long-ago days?

For these are but a few of the countless thousands of ways that life, as it is lived and expressed by each individual, lives and regenerates itself in common cyclic patterns from out his past. And how can we temper the evil of tomorrow, knowing that all that is good and evil of today will thus so regenerate itself. Of what good are our educational systems, our political fronts, our various interpretations, interpolations and integrations of all the various known elements of this life when they can be so considered as merely resurgent patterns and expressions? And as they have doomed the people and their civilizations of the past, so will they doom the future, just as we in the present are finding this same enigmatic doom.

Hasten then the day when the Radiant Light of introspection will contain all that is necessary for man to see his past, present and future; for knowledge of the past, in constructive usage of the present combined with certain directive and progressive elements of the Infinite Mind, will enable man to see his future—a future free from the pestilence, greed and destruction of the material life.

*Now in the year 1971, with the reprinting of this book, these percentages have been stepped up immeasurably. — ("Today at the turn of the century the figures are even more appalling".)

CHAPTER 8

Psychokinesis

In reading through various previous texts, the author is well aware that the reader may have difficulty in understanding the presentation of these concepts; likewise, the reader should understand that the author has difficulty in coining into words, these various higher abstractions; for the vocabulary of any language is justifiable in its usage and these abstractions, being extremely complex in nature, go beyond the ordinary dimensions currently expressed in our present-day lexicon.

Therefore, any presentations which are not completely analogous to the nature of the text are as forgivable as are the misunderstandings which may occur with the reader in the process of mental digestion; and on this basis, therefore, we shall turn the gem of Truth from side to side that it may present its many and different facets to you.

In this way, through persistence in your efforts to understand, infiltration of wisdom is inevitable. Persistence therefore is the keynote. Equitable understanding always occurs when suitable harmonic relationships are set up within the reader's mind. By now, it should also be obvious to the reader that as a seeker of Truth he has been attracted to and has some knowledge of various mind science groups which, small or large, have combined within themselves certain tenets of mental perspectives which are to some degree apparently similar in nature; these we are discussing in these texts. Perhaps the reader, too, can enumerate specific examples of apparent demonstrations, or knows of others who have done so.

As we have unintentionally and without malice or forethought drawn these groups into the vortex of analysis, let us therefore go more properly into that field of mental expression called (by some) mind science, but which should more properly be classified as psychokinesis.

The subject (psychokinetics) in itself is one of vast and broad implications and will be dealt with properly in other texts. The so-called mind scientist, however, knows little or nothing of psychokinesis, nor is he concerned with the mechanics behind autosuggestive, self-hypnotic malpractices, all of which are part of any mind science which uses daily affirmations or concentrations on good aspects, this classification to which prayer also properly belongs.

For prayer is one of the oldest forms of mental malpractice and which seemingly has been the first step in which aboriginal earth people took their first steps toward self-realization. However, by what name we call all mental function, it is more understandable when it is first reduced to the one common form of expression which is not only scientific in nature but is best understood as it should be, a complete science.

Subdivisions of various mind science groups and their tenets are also more properly understood; likewise, we will more properly begin to understand that psychokinesis as well as other forms of mental gymnastics such as mind reading, clairvoyance, predictive ability to see either the past, present or future and can all be scientifically rationalized and made acceptable to our modern classical sciences. When we begin to obtain proper perspectives and realizations in the actual mechanics involved, then indeed, all religions including Christianity and their deviations known as mind sciences will appear primitive and elemental in nature.

The reader therefore, must realize that it makes little difference in what direction he begins to analyze, how he would subdivide or fractionalize various expressive forms of life about him, whether his objectivism is animate or inanimate, he must first reduce all such apparent forms into a common constituent —energy. The illusion of mass was "destroyed" by nuclear physics and by Einstein, who first conceived some small part of this truth.

The subject of mass itself, like psychokinesis or any other divisions, has broad and infinite ramifications. Energy therefore becomes the keystone in the arch of understanding. We will therefore begin with the most common expressive form of energy, called by science, the sine wave. This is a certain quotient of energy traveling through space or matter in a manner which can be likened best to a wave traveling across the ocean. It is either a molecular or an atomic transference of energy from any given point to another. To do this it must have two poles. This is necessary because any media through which the wave travels must thus retransfer this energy wave in direct facsimile to other and similar constituents of this media. Positive and negative polarities are therefore used to describe the energy transference contained in the wave frequency. Also necessary to understand, is the number of times this wave repeats itself positively and negatively from its source or EMF. (This is the frequency.)

At this point we must say that herein also enters a very important part of your introspection which is spectra. Spectra is a group of classifications called dimensions. In other words, a dimension roughly comprises energy wave forms which are compatible to one another on the basis of frequency, and the related remanifestation of frequency called harmonics.

Harmonics are more easily understood as energy transferences as follows: when the "A" strings of two violins are tuned exactly, one will resonate when the other is plucked. This is direct energy transference through sympathetic or harmonic repetition of the same frequency structures. Energy from one string in its various and numerous frequencies, called harmonics or overtones, generates wave forms which travel through the air striking the other string, causing it to vibrate. This is a very important concept which science calls ringing. It is especially important when we can visualize that the Infinite Mind (which the religionist might call God), is a vast and incalculable storehouse of power, a huge dynamo, if you would like to picture it as such, which is generating a great and tremendous power.

This power is being broadcast, so to speak, as vortices of energy which, in their proper and allied frequencies, go to make up a large number of dimensions. These dimensions, incidentally, are what the scientist calls space and which is actually infinitely filled with large and small vortices of energy all properly functioning and closely affiliated on the basis of frequency relationships in an infinite number of harmonic expressions.

Man, therefore, can be visualized physically, mentally and spiritually as merely a composite group of energy configurations; and that any functions of this man, physical or mental, is only an interception or regeneration of these principles and function on the same basis of energy wave forms and associated harmonic patterns.

It must be remembered at this point that any sine wave or energy manifestation which can be pictured as a sine wave, carries a definite bit of information and any wave form carries this information in the manner and way in which it is shaped or fashioned. A wave form can be square; it can have various configurations and distortions throughout its entire form. It can even carry numerous other wave forms piggyback, so to speak, within itself. These various configurations, convolutions or distortions are repeated throughout its entire length; in other words we can say, through the wave form chain, from its beginning to its end (unless otherwise changed from some other outside source harmonically attuned, or by the source itself), can transfer its idiom of intelligence or information on the basis of frequency, to any other wave forms or energy configurations, which are called atoms or otherwise, provided proper conditions of attunement or frequency relationships have been met.

Now that we have plunged, so to speak, into the great unknown world of the higher science, the reader will begin to slightly understand the infinite nature of the Infinite. He should also begin to understand (as suggested), that he see his life about him in whatever manner or form it presents itself, that while he may see this as the great illusion of mass working in the customary reactionary patterns, yet behind the scenes, so to speak, these immutable principles are functioning.

Yes, even the five senses must function according to these principles: the transference of energy forms from one particular dimension of prospection to another. To see physically, merely means we intercept certain wave forms of energy relayed to the proper brain cells, which are actually transducers or transistors. They, in turn, transform these energy impulses into frequencies which are compatible to the psychic or spiritual body where again the ringing or regenerative process takes place.

Likewise, all atoms in the human body are properly attuned through their electromagnetic fields to this psychic energy anatomy and, as a part of this ringing, or regenerative process, the physical body constantly re-creates itself according to the intelligence quotients which are contained in each wave form. This is an automatic process and one in which the individual has very little, if any, control. Any such control in the process of automatic physical regeneration takes place indirectly and as a process of harmonic relationship through the various psychic and physical centers.

Therefore to the reader who is beginning to understand these principles, the various religions, mind science groups and such, and in their understanding and their expression thereof, are quite primitive and elemental in nature and even the scientist has, to this present day, only a primitive science which still relegates and holds him to the material and animal-like dimensions in which he has begun his first evolution.

To date, to the scientist the mysteries of the atom or the mysteries of the human mind are almost as great as they were in the days when the scientist first started his evolution and they will continue to puzzle and confound him, along with many other mysteries of life, until that day of personal emancipation when he frees his mind from the limited boundaries of terrestrial introspection; when he can conceive the Infinite as the source and that his earthly domain or physical world is but one of the infinite number of ways which are manifest in this Infinity, he will stop trying to equate the sum and total of all this Infinity on the basis of his 101 elements and their relationship to him.

Likewise, the religionist will cease to personalize these expressions of Principle of the Infinite, calling them various gods or God. He will begin to see the function of Principle in all things. He will cease to utter useless prayers to these fancied deities. His dreams of heaven, intercession from earthly sins, etcetera, will all vanish as childish fairy stories when he can visualize that the pathway of life is a continuance of expression to any individual and one which could lead him in proper sequence from one dimension to another, leaving behind various kinds of worlds which he may have inhabited for thousands of lifetimes and epochs of time. He will again enter into a new cycle of living, a new way of expressing finitely in his own niche of life, more of these infinite forms of expression which are radiating from the great Source. This then, is life; classify it as you wish. All ways are but forms of expression wherein the individual may polarize through experience, the facsimile of this experience in the Higher Self.

All classifications are thus but steps, points of realization toward the ultimate but never attained goal; a goal which can be only partially achieved in any dimension and complete achievement lies beyond the horizon of comprehension.

Let us now turn our attention upon what is perhaps the most important concept which relates any individual in his earth life dispensations and such expressive relationships with the Infinite—that of psychokinesis—that field of mental endeavor wherein the earthman begins to learn of a more direct mental function with the Infinite. For as it has been so conceived that through proper progressive evolution any individual ultimately becomes a participating, creative element with the Infinite.

The field of psychokinesis embraces all such expressive forms of mental prerogatives which acknowledge higher so-called mystical forces. In this expressive group is found all of the numerous religions of the world; their various ceremonies, prayers and meditations being the first steps taken in which mind energies begin to be directed into specific areas of human relationships. This is true of the witch doctor in the jungle, the priest in the temple or any and all Christian groups of religious expressions.

In almost all cases, these different groups and their

function as expressive elements in directing these higher and comparatively unknown forces to the betterment of mankind—and the individual in particular—do so with one common ingredient, that of symbology.

Through symbolic forms and the associated protocol of any particular group, numerous intercessive prayers are offered up to the various reigning deities or configurations in the hope that these forces will be sufficiently intimidated to lend the desired aid. In the light of higher introspection, it can be considered that while these first steps are essential and necessary in progressive evolution, yet they are entirely primitive and elemental and the underlying principle is in no wise understood.

This accounts for the lack of man's success, or his failure to achieve the desired results in his efforts; for individually or collectively, while some small or large fraction of success may be achieved in one instance, there are large and untold numbers of such prayerful supplications which bear no fruit whatsoever, and whose sole benefit lies in temporarily discharging certain static psychic pressures; but the attendant relief, an age-old escape mechanism, is again functioning.

There are at least two mentions in the New Testament, and utterances of certain individuals which imply that psychokinesis was understood by several of the ancient Adepts who have taught humanity in one form or another. Jesus said, "When two or more are gathered together in My name," again referring to a certain dynamic principle of expressive motion between two or more polarities, (oscillation).

Remember, however, the direct reference to the self or personal pronoun is a misinterpretation of those who followed after and transcribed His teachings and life. The personal pronoun with which He always referred to Himself, must always be carried into a more direct connotation with the Higher or Superconscious Self and its function with the Infinite. It is this Principle which is applied and functions with any group of individuals who are joined in a common union of purpose.

To better understand the principle of psychokinesis, whether it concerns singular expressive forms, or in such group formations which we might find in churches or various public gatherings, let us first carry our introspection from this third or earthly dimension into a more proper starting place—several of the nearby and unknown dimensions. There we will begin to see and understand that the earth and all its expressive forms of animate or inanimate life, whether compounded or dynamically expressed and motivated, are only surface manifestations of a vast and complex interdimensional system of an infinite number of expressive forms of energy which are part of the Infinite Mind.

In this superabundant, energy-filled cosmos called space, man's various expressive forms of life are seen to be merely points of interception, wherein man succeeds in relaying the desired creative forms, a certain small fraction of infinite expression. As of this time, mankind in general, has not yet learned this principle but has amassed a vast and preponderant system of various expressive third dimensional forms, hoping and striving to solve the unknown riddle from this third dimensional way of life.

Let us now focus our attention upon one of the segments of human relationship with the Infinite which is directly concerned in the interplay of the mind with the Higher dimensions, the little known but much practiced art of divine healing; for it can be said, that in almost any instance wherein the danger of death is imminent for an individual, prayer or individual intercession is almost always entered into by those who are more directly concerned with this individual when other means have failed. This, of course, refers to the various functions of the priests, ministers or practitioners who are supposedly able to carry on intercession more proficiently than the so-called untrained individual; yet how little do these practitioners know of their art or science.

First, let us consider the great principle of life. All forms of energy in any way or manner in which they are so expressed into the material world from other, or higher dimensions, do so in this manner: time is an integrated factor of relationship with energy in these higher dimensional forms, wherein all such energy forms thus become individual, self-contained expressions, revolving in cyclic paths and linked one to another through frequency, or its harmonics. Energy, to express itself in the third or material dimension, must separate itself from the time element so that time becomes the unit of self in the expressive form. This energy must then travel in a straight line configuration to attain separation from its time content; it does this by traveling from one given point to another at the speed of light which is 186,000 miles per second.

Energy transduction is always thus so expressed in this time separation. This is true with the building and maintaining of any physical form or the function of any part or cell therein. This is the purpose of the atoms which are the constituents of various cell structures, for each atom is a transducer of energy from the higher dimensions into the various compound structures of the human body. This is done according to the base plane rate of every atom. All atoms are linked one to another into molecules and cells etcetera, through their electromagnetic fields, and all energy so expressed in the human body does so in this time separation principle.

Let us take a more specific example so that we may better understand natural or divine healing. In the case of a broken leg bone, time mandates a period of several months before bone cell structures have so joined the broken ends together. However, the same bone could be healed instantly and in specific examples, such as are mentioned in the new Testament, many healing miracles concerning other kinds of body malfunctions or diseases were performed in this manner. The mind of the practitioner concerned with the healing could concentrate and direct from the other, or higher side of life, sufficient intelligent energy or forces into the energies which were stemming into the body in their natural sequence; time could thus be separated at the source, so to speak, and the necessary energy in atomic forms could be expressed instantly into the specified areas, such as the broken ends of the bone, where such energy would immediately assume its correct atomic form and subsequent formation of bone cell structures, thus an instant knitting of the bone.

There are numerous instances in history, Biblical and otherwise, where instantaneous healings have been achieved; and in many cases where such individual practitioners were responsible for such healings, they understood, at least partially, this principle.

To the countless millions however, who practice prayer or some other psychokinetical form, this is a hit or miss situation, the chances being 1000 or more to one against their success in achieving the necessary alignment in these higher dimensions wherein mind energies can be so directed as to separate time from the wellspring of energy as it flows into the human body.

Yes, for even in the simple act of eating food, there is a certain definite element of psychokinetics which, through long association in past lifetimes, the individual has learned to use, in various bodily functions, the transference from one form of energy to another in what is called the chemistry of the body; for this chemistry is indeed only another process wherein the fourth dimensional (or source) energy re-manifests itself in the desired form and functions in the human body.

It must be remembered, however, that psychokinetics, whether understood or misunderstood by the earth plane man, should never be used as a substitute for an even higher principle of life; for the benefits of spiritual healing through any agency or expression thereof, as a psychokinetical process, does seldom if ever, correct malformed psychic structures which are always directly the cause of almost any known or unknown disease in the body.

In the process of corrective therapy as it concerns subpsychic structures which are malformed or aberrated, psychokinetics must be transferred from its point of function in the conscious mind to the Superconscious. In the realization of a higher directive or expressive form of intelligence from this Superconscious, the individual thus makes his conscious mind subservient to such action as the Superconscious may take in directing corrective or healing measures into the psychic substructures.

It now becomes quite evident that in this higher process of function, the conscious or external mind becomes the transducer, just as does the atom in the body structures; conscious mind thus implying itself in the necessary requisites which make corrective energy transferable into the psychic substructures. Here again is the inalienable prerogative of the individual in the expression of self, which is so necessary in attaining that much-desired and long-sought-after direct functioning with the Infinite Mind.

Spiritual or divine healing, therefore can be said to be an expressive condiment in any individual's life, only after he has prepared himself for its usage in the higher dimensions; for indeed, as there is a life on earth for everyone, there is also a life in between these earth lives; a spiritual life wherein certain comparatively more advanced individuals begin to learn and understand these principles. Man's desire to return to earth therefore becomes mandated not only to work out existing shock experiences called karma, but to work out these karmic conditions on the basis of his newly acquired knowledge, and in the full realization of its meaning to him, the attainment of more complete knowledge and practice.

However, this knowledge and its usage does not come in one spiritual life or in one earth life. Such knowledge and proper usage in practice will come only after living many thousands of such lives, for in the individual mind, expressive forms of energy are subdivided into infinitely small portions called experiences. This Infinite again re-creates itself from these experiences through polarization of the Higher Self of the individual, which again expresses Infinity through expressive psychokinetics or directive transference of intelligent motion as a creative substance and force, into all subdivisions which need this creative expression.

Again we say, do not concentrate on attaining any spiritual healing; release the conscious mind from such concentrated blockage; make it passive and subservient by viewing Infinity through the Superconscious. Holding the mind in complete contact with the Higher Self is necessary before corrective measures can take place.

If you do not obtain such corrective therapy, there is either misalignment or the Higher Self, in its position to view the past and future, may know that you need the value of experience as is contained from whatever you are presently wishing to be healed; and that you would be cheating yourself from great benefits which could be realized in that polarization process of experience.

Life is Infinite and you need not be emotionally

concerned with the present moment because each moment is not valuable to you in the terms of a long lifetime, but only in the polarization derived and extracted from the various forms of expressive motion which are passing through these moments. For, in the future eons of time, your ability to live and function in a higher dimension or way of life will depend upon polarized abstractions of these experiences.

CHAPTER 9

Education — A Fantasy?

Every year colleges, universities and high schools graduate many thousands of young men and women who, according to these ranks, are educated. It is well known however, that most of these graduates are absorbed into various strata of social life and apparently have not fully justified either the claims made by educators or by any such personal exemplifications of brilliance or genius which could be attributed as a culminating realization of our educational systems.

Moreover, in almost all cases, such education relegated this individual within the strict precincts of that particular curriculum from which he graduated; he possesses only mental automation, a parrot-like configuration of form and substance which suggests that the individual is incapable of mental spontaneity, independent action, or such mental functions and their usages which could be considered independently creative. Psychologically speaking, this obvious fact is substantiated, inasmuch as a close study of mental processes reveals the obvious fact that any person is merely correlating past existent forms of consciousness from the subconscious into the present tense.

It is also widely known and almost without exception, that any and all advances, discoveries and inventions in the broad field of our present-day technocracy, were discovered "accidentally" in one way or another. The direct application of existing human knowledge has very seldom been sufficient to conclude a direct approach upon some intangible objective. The inefficiency of our educational systems and failure to meet existing demands is quite well known to educators and other people who are interested in public welfare and, in contrast to our supposedly high educational standards, we have the greatest mental health problem which has faced any nation and which could indeed be the one dominant factor which would eventually and inevitably destroy our way of life.

The ramifications and implications here, however, are vast and broad and go into such associated fields as could be called metaphysical or religious in nature. The whole and conglomerate mass of humanity which lives under the American flag is a vast melting pot of many nations—a matrix of humanity compounded from every race and creed upon the face of the globe.

While the tenets of democracy are theoretically broad enough to encompass these various ways of life, there are, however, great psychic tensions which are always generated under such conditions. For the future therefore, our educational systems must be changed and reoriented to include such metaphysical factors which will help alleviate the background of racial differences. Such idealisms that all people are created equal are not sufficient—individually or collectively—to discharge these psychic tensions.

As for the purpose of education, in its pure esoterical sense this means that the student not only studies and subconsciously remembers the usual curriculum, but that he is given direct knowledge and practice which will give him independent thought and action and create an intelligent mental perspective which functions beyond the horizons of the commonly accepted curricular boundaries.

For mankind to understand this better process of learning, which will give the individual student this independent integrated action and which will make of him a creative mentality, such teaching will have to include certain elements of human behavior which are presently not known by either educators, or any so-called scientific dispensations.

In these various texts, there will be very adequately described these various additional perspectives which will give to our educational systems, when included, the necessary knowledge which could conceivably make creative minds out of many thousands who have been deprived of this expressive life under existing educational systems.

It must be thoroughly understood that there is a great difference between true learning and the subconscious retentive memory process which is presently called learning, for this memory process is a "cut and dried" situation which seldom, if ever, correctly attunes the individual to his own individual psychic constituents. True learning is a process whereby the knowledge to be learned must first be visualized as thought train wave forms containing the desired information. Through the known or unknown senses which link every person to this evolution of life, these thought train wave forms must be attuned properly so that when they are reflected into, or oscillate with the individual's subconscious, these individual wave train constituents will so catalyze or regenerate, not only in the subconscious psychic structures but in other adjunctive psychic structures as well; this catalyzing or regeneration thereby canceling out and rebuilding, as well as polarizing, these various necessary psychic structures which will then give this individual a complete psychic rapport or attunement with the Higher Self in the perspective of knowledge which has caused this regenerative and rebuilding process.

The individual can now use this higher form of attunement to properly align this knowledge with the Infinite perspective. This alignment will, in turn through the Superconscious, regenerate any number of wave train configurations which are thus pertinent to or objectively combined with the original existing information, which so prompted this higher reactive process.

The individual can now be said to possess independent creative thought inasmuch as he is using the mind as an integrator to subtract into consciousness the various necessary elements which exist in the Infinite Mind; and he is not dependent upon the comparatively limited subconscious content which is compounded from past life experiences (or educational symposiums).

When this principle is thoroughly understood and included in our future educational systems, then indeed we shall foster a race of mental giants, many of whom will be, in the idiom of common understanding as much, or more than the Biblical characters who purveyed life and healing to many people. This future race will live, not by the primitive laws of survival of the fittest, an eye for an eye and a tooth for a tooth, but will live individually and collectively as expressive units of Infinite Consciousness, and that future day could be the long-sought-after Utopia—the religionist's heaven—for the very nature of this man has been changed; subconscious reactive elements, destructive both in recreation and re-expression, will have polarized their idiom of knowledge in the higher superpsychic structures; then with their destructive content discharged, and with this discharging of the old materialistic subconscious, man thus cuts the last ties which bind him to material earth—breaks the fetters and chains with which he has bound himself to the wheel of karma.

Yet sadly enough, all this will not be done in one man's life, nor of the many years in the future which lie ahead of the peoples of the earth; for well it is, in the eye of the Infinite, that this earth is a school of learning and discipline; a place of many grades or elevations of life, all a comparatively primitive scale of human evolution. And as this little speck of cosmic dust turns in its little cycle, these people of the earth come and go through many portals, just as they have for almost countless thousands of years; and as they reach certain thresholds of understanding, they pass on into other worlds, some higher some lower, to again take up this cyclic path of evolution, acting and reacting from the knowledge previously gained either destructively or that they have now become one of the more fortunate who has learned to be creatively select-ive with the Infinite Mind.

CHAPTER 10

Automation — Or Sanity?

Now that we have made certain objective comparisons between subconscious or reactionary thinking and the higher and more desirable element of creative thinking, the attainment of such idealisms in our educational systems for the future generations would quite naturally have to include many concepts of life which are comparatively unknown to the masses of our materialistic sophisticates of this age of automation.

It is well to remember that these concepts were understood and used in child training and development in several unrecorded and almost forgotten civilizations of the past; concepts which have only survived the long ages and which appear today in certain areas of the world in a deleted symbolic form, usually associated with certain religious expressions.

For instance, the present ruling Dalai Lama in Tibet was chosen when, as a child, he met certain rigid test conditions set up by his predecessor before his death. These tests were of such nature as to dramatically demonstrate reincarnation. In other words, the former Dalai Lama is now the present person occupying a new and different body and these tests precluded the possibility of any errors which might arise. In this way, therefore, the present reigning Lama can carry on his beneficent reign, just as he formerly did, with all the attendant advantages and their connotions as he so expressed them in the former lives and in the same capacity.

A moments thought would quickly point out the advantages such knowledge would give leading nations of the world in their more highly advanced technocracy. Yes, the scientists, politicians, public leaders, educators, artists, musicians and a thousand more such adopted expressionists of life, which could be called highly developed, would be much more proficient and prolific if carried on in the understanding and usage, that through evolution or reincarnation these certain expressive individuals would thus be enabled to sustain from life to life, a more proficient and advanced expression of their selected profession.

Indeed, it may be that this has to some degree been subconsciously acknowledged, for in certain areas of our country, educational systems, during the past decade, tried to approach the problem of better education in a manner in which they believed to be a psychological inference but which was actually basically motivated by past lifetime expressions of these educators wherein there were affiliations of knowledge with this evolutionary system. We are making reference to that pattern of education which is referred to as the non-inhibitive form.

In other words, every child from kindergarten is given a rather loose uninhibited prerogative in choosing various constituents of his education. In this system he can indulge himself rather freely in various classroom activities, the belief being that he will soon thus automatically select his best vocational aptitudes. Later on, in the teen-age groups, various agencies or bodies have been set up in most schools for the expressed purpose of vocational guidance; the emphasis here being placed on specialization.

However, this system has been only partially successful; as a matter of fact, many parent groups are urging its cessation, for it has been found that many children begin to develop a licentious usage of this uninhibitive psychology and some of the country's foremost thinkers believe that it is presently aggravating, or is responsible for a great part of the present-day, teen-age crime wave, dope addiction and juvenile delinquency.

Indeed this is so, when we understand psychic affiliations with past lifetimes. Because a child in kindergarten seems to be attracted to the art of painting, does not necessarily mean that this child has a latent precocity for it, for all such latent precocities are not the commonly supposed gifts or talents but are actually developments of long standing, embracing not only expression in many past lifetimes in a like manner and form, but must also include spiritual training accumulated in the lives between earth lives in more highly developed spiritual worlds where this certain individual finds his accustomed expression in a much more highly developed form.

The child in kindergarten therefore, who tries to paint, may do so purely because in one or more past lifetimes he was a servant in some large castle or chateau wherein his master had accumulated a great wealth of various art forms, including paintings by various masters. On the basis of personal acquisitiveness and reasons of personal security, greed, longing —the servant coveted this art, and so great was his desire that several hundred years later as a child in one of our modern, present-day kindergartens, he would try to recreate these strong subconscious desires. This is indeed quite different than the training acquired by the masters who had created these coveted paintings and that they had spent many thousands of years in this expressive development before they were enabled to express a relative degree of achievement. Moreover, the greatness in any painting—or in any creation for that matter—does not necessarily lie within the strict dimension of its construction, but this greatness is found and expressed in all such manners and forms of art when the creator is able to interject a higher and unknown quality of energy (a form of psychokinesis), which will subsequently always attune, in a form of transcendency, those who view this work of art and are so suitably indoctrinated in certain perspectives of art from past lifetimes.

This will easily explain why some people like art and others find little or no use for it. The connections here are strictly psychic in nature and attuned to such various forms of energy which are contained in the subconscious portions of each individual's psychic body; and whether it is art, or any one of a thousand other different vocations and associated expressions, the principle holds true and is inviolate.

Therefore, for the future, if we are to evolve or develop a constructive educational system, it must include these tenets: that every child of kindergarten age undergo a scientific analysis of his various attributes and propensities, based primarily upon training and expression achieved in former lifetimes. This analysis and subsequent correct placement of the child will automatically eliminate abnormal tendencies psychically based on past lifetime experiences which can be considered negative or destructive in nature.

Further suppression and eventual cancellation of such abnormal tendencies can be further expedited on the basis of this same past life analysis. Then by the time the child has entered teenage years, he will not need vocational guidance, for by that time, he will have entered into a more highly developed expression of his particular vocation as was so expressed in former lives.

It might be well to point out that this would not necessarily lead mankind into eventual specialized automation, for no human being can support any singular expression in his life to the exclusion of all others. However, any singular expression, as a vocation or avocation, (and that such expression is highly specialized), is thus attained only as a conjunctive point of self or personal realizations which have thus culminated and found, in the common and highly developed expression, the focal point of expression, for the individual so concerned in his conjunction with the Higher Self and the Infinite Mind.

Such highly developed expressionists can therefore be found to have many multiple expressions of life, all creative and indicative of their mental development and their ability to function with the Higher Self, and the Higher Planes of life. Leonardo da Vinci was one of these, and, aside from being a master painter, his autobiography reveals hundreds of inventions such as the airplane, helicopter, motors—hundreds of years ahead of their time. And the same picture holds true in all individual cases wherein this individual has, with his mind, created a pliant substance and, in many and diversified forms, has created various configurations of the Infinite Mind.

In the future day when our educational systems are so functioning and include these various expressive concepts, then indeed we shall be building a new civilization, the religionists' "New City of Jerusalem", the Buddhists' "Nirvana" and at least part of any deistic attainments which are so contained in various religions or pantheisms. The man of today must, by necessity, make his position more secure in his future evolutions upon this earth by beginning to include and develop such inclusions—the various elements of evolution and personal development—which are pertinent and of vital concern to every individual. Such inclusions, and their development, will be the master stroke to cut the Gordian knot of our present day civilization and its many insoluble enigmas.

Sufficient to say, that of this time and place, as our

civilization is so currently expressed, it is either unaware, or is a non-practicing agent, of this scientific evolutionary understanding of life; as a consequence there are no psychic diagnosticians who could so analyze children by their past lifetime experiences. And as there is neither concept nor usage, its development and usage might well become a question asked in that age-old riddle, "which came first, the hen or the egg?" And the answer, ridiculous as the riddle may seem, is quite intelligent and embraces all known and 'unknown' elements of progressive, cyclic evolution whether it concerns an individual or a civilization.

To the future, therefore, to the new educational system and to the psychic diagnostician who will replace our present-day psychologist—like each man who rises and salutes his new day—so we, too, salute the new tomorrow, a day not fettered or bound by the unknown yesterday but, in the knowing of that yesterday, we have also found new strength in the purpose and achievement in the solution of that yesterday; a new strength which carries us forward through the dawn of our new day and into the many days which follow.

CHAPTER 11

Secret Mysteries — Debunked

Have you ever been sold a "bill of goods" about some great secret mystery teaching taught by some self-deified Master? No doubt you have; most Truth seekers have subscribed to at least one or more of these pseudo cults, and like the others, you have laid down cold hard cash for these so-called teachings and have ended up disappointed, disillusioned, your faith unjustified.

Children live in a make-believe world—a world of fantasy where they realistically play various adult roles. This is a common escape mechanism used by children to relieve psychic pressures generated in orienting themselves in their new earth life environment.

Adults, too, have their own world of fantasy. Common living methods and habits generate psychic pressures, deflations of the ego, compromises and guilts and when compounded with misunderstood movements of natural forces around them, intensify these psychic pressures which demand relief; such relief usually being found in various diversions used by most people. Cigarettes, getting drunk, movies, television, hobbies and vacations are common relief valves; and heading the list of all escape mechanisms is religion. This applies to all past and present dispensations including Christianity.

A person suffering from unrelieved psychic pressures becomes an easy victim of the wolves and vampires who prey upon this fringe-like segment of humanity. These ghoulish creatures are found in all therapeutic practices such as medicine, psychology, politics, purveyors as well as religion, and as of today these monsters are in much greater affluence and abundance than in any other past historical time.

It is much easier to believe in "divine intercession", remission of sins, salvation, than to shoulder one's own personal, moral responsibilities and to acknowledge the fact that he, himself, is the primary cause for his present suffering and, under such conditions, such a person is easily mesmerized into swallowing —hook, line and sinker—various garbled and distorted versions of some supposedly great emancipating "belief" which will eventually whisk him away on a pink cloud to heaven where he will live a life of indolence and ease.

Such beliefs are not only unrealistic, but more properly belong in the realm of fantasy and should be classified as fairy stories, myths and fables and which could be conceived as true only by those who were extremely neurotically ill. The fact of the matter is —there are no great hidden or secret mysteries; all great Adepts and Avatars who have visited and taught upon this earth stressed the same cardinal principle of life.

Buddha taught the junction of mind with the higher spiritual self and its position to the great invisible cosmogony; this is called Nirvana. Jesus taught the same principle; in other words, "The Kingdom of Heaven Within", and the Father or Christ Self, or the Higher Superconscious Entity which everyone possesses and which dwells in that Kingdom. These principles are as badly misunderstood today as they were in the time when these respective individuals taught them, for these Adepts were restricted by the common level of intelligence expressed by their followers.

As a matter of fact, as of today, the average high school student has a better understanding of life and the visible world about him than all of the other so-called self-styled teachers and adepts, disciples, prophets who followed after these few Masters. This also holds true in regard to the various scientists, literates, teachers of the past ages. The average boy or girl knows more about astronomy than did Galileo or Copernicus. The high school graduate has a better philosophical and psychological understanding than did many of the expressionists who followed men like Socrates, Plato, and Aristotle.

The truth of the matter is as was previously said—there is no such thing as a great hidden mystery. The great Infinite Creative Mind is ever and always about us; it is the substance of all visible and invisible things and is just as easily understood by one person as it is by another, provided he possesses the necessary fortitude, dedication and purpose to learn of the Infinite, to achieve a Higher Way of life and has had previous conditioning.

To learn of and to achieve a more advanced mode of living which will be comparatively free from the insoluble earth life vicissitudes, mandates that such a person who so wishes to achieve, must first strip himself, so to speak, of all such dogmatic creeds and systems with which he has, in the past, been associated. He must place these things where they most properly belong, in the past, useful only to those who have not yet found a way to solve the various differences of life through logic, reason and understanding.

If this person is so minded to live a higher way of life, he must also realize the infinite proportions of this vast Creative Mind and substance which the religionists call God or gods and he must not attempt, in any way, to place his stamp of approval or disapproval according to the bias of his opinions, or in any way circumscribe this great Creative Intelligence within the confines of his own understanding. For such action always limits this person to his own past experiences and is in no way conducive to attaining a progressive evolution which leads to the Higher Way.

In the past ages there were many and various mystery schools and mystic cults; the proponents of these systems muttered the same symbolic mumbo-jumbo to their adherents as do the proponents and expressionists of present-day mystery schools and mystic cults. These schools and cults include all known forms of religion including Christianity, for this religion is just as much of a mystery school or mystic cult as any practiced in the barbaric and pagan past.

There is only one way to achieve a better life; first, the possibility must be conceived; second, the necessity for such a life as common participation in the dynamic evolutionary principle of life; third, actual knowledge of this advanced life, where and how it is to be lived, environmental conditions, influences, systems or other such social impedimenta which are classically associated with life.

Such preconditioning demands thorough and basic knowledge of the Infinite, beyond the horizon of various earth life creeds and dogmas and other such associated religions and scientific dispensations. And how else could anyone achieve a higher life without such a reasonable approach? For no one can live in an environment which is foreign to his nature and which he does not understand.

If, therefore, you wish to achieve the Higher life, begin now to prepare yourself. This can be done by first acquainting yourself with the basic principles of science which are partially contained in various scientific dispensations at this present time; also seek out the meaning and purpose of all things which are presently beyond your understanding. Also seek out the hidden psychic or spiritual evolution which propagates and engenders all forms of life about you. A tiny seed, a flower, a tree, all forms and objects which are everywhere about you—all carry this "hidden" meaning; and in their earth life, are expressing the common psychic or spiritual constituents which are indigenous to all things.

All of these necessary constituents are contained in the scientific teachings of Unarius. The various books, lesson courses, etcetera, present a straight line method of achieving all of the necessary ingredients which will start you on your way toward a better life.

Unarius should not be misconstrued as another mystery cult school, for the basic principles contained in these teachings are the same used by various modern sciences of this day. This present-day science is used as a foundation to combine various other more advanced perspectives which concern the great Infinite microcosm and macrocosm which is just beginning to be explored by our present-day scientists.

With Unarius, the teaching of Jesus most applicable here is "By their fruits ye shall know them", and the files of Unarius contain thousands of wonderful testimonials written in gratitude by those whose lives have been changed; their mental and physical illnesses and obsessions of all kinds have vanished into the realm of memory.

These people are from all walks and all ages of life; a few are doctors and scientists, others are hardly literate, yet with the proper elements of preconditioning in spiritual worlds and other lives combined with a great necessity, purpose and faith from this inward knowing, they have been able basically to master the principles of life as they are contained in the science of Unarius. And from their particular point of emancipation, they will now be enabled to travel forward and upward in their pathway to the higher spiritual worlds.

However, as it could be with you, just as it is with

these people, do not look for an immediate and quick achievement; in fact, the road ahead will be long and difficult. It will take you countless thousands of years to achieve a better way; for as each better way is realized, this in turn will become only a platform for an even greater achievement and higher way.

This is the way of life, the so-called "Divine Plan" which the Infinite Creative Intelligence has planned for all of us; nor shall we ever arrive at any terminating point of our forward and upward evolution, providing we have the necessary incentive, realization and purpose.

CHAPTER 12

The Clarion Call

Two thousand years ago, a man walked along the shore of an inland sea. He was tall and of red beard and hair, and of noble bearing; yet there was much more than this which set Him apart from all others. And as He walked, He came upon a boat resting on the beach wherein sat two fishermen, mending their nets. And He called to them saying, "Come, follow me, I will make you fishers of men." And straightaway they laid down their nets and followed.

What kind of courage was this that could cause these two to follow this unknown stranger? Perhaps it was an inward knowing that superseded any natural desires or instincts to remain with the known things of their life. And as they followed, the day quickly came when they were vindicated in this apparent madness and they saw many miracles wrought and great Truths spoken.

And there were others, too, who likewise followed, and saw, and heard. And many fell by the wayside, for they could not meet the one simple requirement which must be fully met with—to give freely of themselves. And of the Twelve who remained and gave of themselves, yet there was even one among these few who would soon sell himself and the others, for thirty pieces of silver; and for this, in his great sorrow, he would hang himself on the thorn tree.*

What great paradox is this; what great mystery is this that always men must turn upon those who love them the most? How often it is that those Great Souls from the Higher Planes have asked Themselves this same question. Yet surely They must know the answer—for indeed it is so, theirs is a never-ending quest to seek goodness and virtue among men in these earthly worlds; and in this quest, finding one and then another who has this goodness and virtue and can give freely of himself; for therein, in this great mystery, lies the answer, sought by all yet found by so few. Yes, even after thousands of years of turmoil and strife among themselves and with their selves, they come not upon the answer and their cries of despair are heard in the Higher places.

And again it is that a white-winged Messenger brings one small flame of Light to lead these few from out of their darkness, for in the Infinite Mind, all things have been conceived, and, in this conception, the fruit of Wisdom is always borne from out of the womb of time wherein all men suffer until the day of their delivery. How great it is to know of this Light and this Fruit, and to know of Him who brings it forth into the darkened regions of these earthly worlds. Yet even greater it is to hold this same Light even though those He came to help would set upon Him like ravening beasts. For as each man is born, truly it is that he liveth not until he liveth for all men.

*According to the King James version of the Bible. However, the manner of Judas' death differs in "The True Life of Jesus", by Alexander Smyth, which is the authentic story, republished by Unarius Publishers.

CHAPTER 13

Giving Freely of Self

In various texts which have been given, there has been frequent mention of a certain phrase, "To Give Freely of Himself." Lest this be misinterpreted, or that it could be used by some person with a strong escape mechanism to vindicate his own mental objectivisms, this particular phrase will therefore be more fully explained.

To give freely of himself does not mean that this person should lay his neck, so to speak, upon any chopping block which might come his way, or that in giving freely is a means of atonement for any sense of guilt such a person may have. Giving freely of himself means simply this: all objectivisms, mental or physical, all concepts and all perspectives of life are carried beyond the horizon of the individual's subconscious, reactionary self. In other words, all mental functions and their relative physical manifestations are an oscillating process carried on with the Higher or Superconscious Self. This is a two-way, back-and-forth transference of energy which will manifest itself in form in the individual's life. In a sense, the individual has thus become a substation of the main power plant wherein this person will transfer such various forms of consciousness as they stem from the Higher or Infinite Self. It should go without saying at this point that such forms of consciousness from the

Higher Self will always be pure expressive forms, completely detached from the stigma of selfhood originating in the subconscious.

There are many and numerous purposes to which this principle should be applied in daily life. The dimension of physical perspectives and its various appurtenances should always be made or manifest from energy which thus stems from the Infinite Source. This is the direct application of a well-known but misunderstood metaphysical law. Giving freely is the right way in which goodness and virtue are made manifest in any individual's life who so understands it correctly. It is not the concentrated effort of sheer will to manifest certain physical objectivisms, as is believed by so many. However the usage of this principle to manifest supply, give guidance, healing assistance isn't the prerogative of the conscious mind which, in itself, is closely affiliated with the old reactionary subconscious. To use this principle, therefore, relaxation of the conscious mind is necessary and made subservient to the higher and more intelligent Superconsciousness. All demonstrations, therefore, will work to conclusion in the individual's life, without his conscious knowledge or without will or effort from his conscious mind.

This is the true attainment and realization of spiritual consciousness and does not begin as is taught by many mind practitioners, materialization by sheer will power. Repetitious sayings, various concentrated efforts with the conscious mind are at best only autosuggestive or hypnotic in nature and their results are very limited and short-lived. Moreover, these concentrated mind practices are but one step removed from age-old practices of witchcraft, black magic, superstition. Therefore, relax the conscious or physical mind and in this atmosphere of relaxation, obstreperous oscillations are temporarily annulled from the subconscious—mind blockages are cancelled out, for attempts at concentration always create static energy which blocks mind functions. In such mental atmosphere of peace and well-being, and secure in the knowledge of the Infinite, the Higher Self can function more freely with the Infinite. You will also be in a much better alignment with the Higher Spiritual plane and the Intelligent Beings who inhabit them and who in turn have a much better working position with the Infinite.

At this point it should be remembered that as you lived through many past lifetimes and countless thousands of experiences are contained therein, these experiences, in turn, have polarized their counterparts or positive facsimiles which are part of the sum and total of this Higher Superconscious Self. This process has created in the Superconscious, various psychic substructures which give this Superconscious its own selfhood in connection with that particular individual. The growth and development of this person's psychic embodiment with any individual depends, quite naturally, upon how many lifetimes he has lived. People who have traveled many thousands of lifetimes therefore have a fairly high degree of development and gradually superseded the function of the conscious mind in its affiliation with the subconscious. Conversely, a person who has lived only a hundred or so lifetimes, is still a very strong materialist and animal-like in nature, depending as he does, on mental function completely as a process sustained from the subconscious.

The various processes as they have just been explained, are the basis for that much misunderstood religious reference to the "Holy Trinity", for this can now clearly be seen to comprise these three elements: the Superconscious Self, or the facsimile of the Infinite, the subconscious or psychic accumulation of the past and the conscious which is merely the integrator.

It is the purpose of each individual in consciousness to gradually transfer the realm of his perspective from the subconscious and attain Spiritual consciousness as a direct rapport of Self with this higher embodiment. This attainment will occur only in that far off, dim and distant future—after passing through countless thousands of earth lives—when the individual has attained this more direct rapport with the Higher Self. He will still retain conscious knowledge of all he has experienced in these countless thousands of lives, (as past memory experiences are contained in the polarized idiom of these Superconscious psychic substructures), but will do so without any reactionary affiliations. In other words, he has attained Mastership and has begun to completely function as a direct cell or unit with the Infinite.

The Infinite Mind is not only the source of all things but is all things. It is each individual's own personal problem to learn how to manifest either mentally, physically or materially such subtractions thereof and how to do this through consciousness, not willpower; consciousness meaning the individual understands the principle involved wherein he is oscillating with, or, in other words, maintaining the correct connections wherein energy from the Infinite flows into consciousness and is polarized or made manifest by action and that this again is returned to the Infinite through the acknowledgment and functioning of principle (polarization).

At this point, it is necessary to interject other adjunctive functions of the principle of "giving one's self", for in the function of this principle with the Infinite, there are an infinite number of ramifications. In other words, no individual supports a singular oscillation, or oscillating condition, with the Infinite. This in itself, would defeat its purpose for the Infinite is not singular. An oscillating condition with the Infinite means that the individual carries on the oscillating condition in an infinite number of ways. This is done through that part of principle known, in the vernacular of the modern-day scientist, as harmonic relationship. In other words, through multiples of approximately two, the consciousness between the Infinite and the individual is thus made possible in an infinite number of ways simply by this regenerative condition of harmonic relationship.

Here again we must interject a word of caution or warning to those who would wrongly use this knowledge for personal benefits. Giving one's self freely, or personal attunement with the Infinite or Superconscious Self, is a scientific principle and best understood as being similar to tuning a radio. Attunement with the Infinite obviously means such infinite abstractions as non-personalized elements manifesting into consciousness. Attempts to personalize or use such abstract elements by abortive methods commonly referred to as demonstration through concentration, will result in not only detuning the individual from the Infinite but such a practice, if carried on long enough, may actually destroy the individual by plunging him deeply into some astral underworlds where he cannot extricate himself. For it must be remembered by every individual, that in the beginning of his evolution man differed from all other plant and animal species in this respect: he was beginning to sustain a progressive pattern of evolution into a higher spiritual form of life by the direct acknowledgment of the Infinite and its function and purpose.

In the beginning of his evolution, therefore, acknowledgment of the Infinite was crude and elemental and took on such expressions and forms which could be called religious in nature. And so, through the various ages and many major and minor civilizations, man symbolized this Infinite in an infinite number of ways by constructing configurations of stone and metal, by conducting various worshipful or votive services and ceremonies—all of which bore tribute to this unknown Infinite in a name and form which the individual could best understand. In this respect, Christianity is no better than any other religion which has gone before it or is currently being expressed, for Christianity is still symbolic in nature and, in this symbology, has erected various configurations and associated protocol which give it the same basic character.

No man can visualize the Infinite in a singular finite mind, for such a mind is only the surface manifestation of various extractions of experiences from many lives which he has lived in the past. To conceive the Infinite, the individual must develop a nonsingular mind, devoid of personal experience extractions —a plural mind, which is capable of realization of the Infinite in an infinite number of ways, simultaneously. Any person is exactly that which he so conceives. Any such person who has developed a plural mind, capable of this infinite function and purpose, can be said to be godlike in nature; that is, if we could personify godlike attributes. However, such a plural mind never functions as a singular person but is always expressing itself Infinitely.

So it was, that while the people of the Holy Land saw the form and figure of the personal man they called Jesus, they did not know—nor do they know today—that that particular individual, as a plural mind, was functioning Infinitely and, in speaking of Himself, was merely referring to the Infinite Self. Perhaps He failed to understand the mental limitations of His followers or whether they would soon understand. Yet we must understand that such expressions of principle as were demonstrated by Jesus, have always been subject to various derelictions and distortions as they are translated into the idiom of personal understanding of any person who follows and attempts to use misunderstood principles for his personal gain and betterment in what might be called the age-old escape mechanism—religion. For religion is, and always has been, such a device—a moral opiate wherein, individually or collectively, people could temporarily relieve the pressures of subconscious guilt complexes.

A much more rational approach to self-realization and the purpose of life will always be one in which the individual realizes the full meaning and implication of the Infinite Mind—his connection unto this Infinite through his Higher Self or Infinite Cell, the ultimate realization in achieving Infinite Introspection, the meaning and purpose of this and the manner in which it is attained. This new meaning and method is not intended as nor should it be used as a substitute for old religions and social systems. It should be visualized as the beginning of ultimate attainment; a beginning which is sometimes called self-realization and to which we have referred as, "giving freely of one's self".

Be patient in attaining self-realization; time has no meaning; only realization is important and, above all, progressive realization. Remember your position in the Infinite perspective. You are tuned either directly or indirectly to all of the subversive reactionary elements of the past and of this world, countless other similar worlds, astral underworlds and to the countless hordes who populate these various centers; or else, through the same attunement (principle), you are attuned directly or indirectly to countless numbers of great spiritual worlds wherein untold and unfathomable numbers of beings live; people who have gone on beyond that threshold of self-realization and are now living without physical bodies, in manner and form which would be impossible to describe and even more impossible to conceive.

In the future eons of time, should your purpose be so sincerely dedicated, you too can live in one of these worlds. May it be one of the Higher Spiritual worlds and may it be that your purpose or lack of it has not carried you in the wrong direction. You will always be —at any given moment—the sum and total of what you can conceive as personal ingredients of consciousness. These ingredients will, quite naturally, determine the environment in which you live. Let us give freely of ourselves—give freely to the Infinite source of all things; and in this giving be filled with the purpose of realization, and in this realization we again regenerate the dynamic purpose of the Infinite.

Unarius Laughs

To the 800 million or so people who call themselves Christians, it can be concluded that many believe quite completely in the moral and literal translation of the Bible. They also believe that this, their present life, is their first and only one. Birth as it is understood by every person is a direct contradiction with the opening chapter of Genesis which says that God made man from the mud of the river bank. This, too, is a contradiction when compared to the creation of Eve who was made from one of Adam's ribs.

If God could make a woman from a rib, why use mud for a man? And by the same token, if the Christian followers believe implicitly in the first creation, then birth by woman is hocus-pocus!

Christian ministers and dispensators of the gospel have been trying to explain this to practical people who would like a practical answer. If God is still creating in the same old manner and fashion, He must be very busy standing on that river-bank making people all day—if present-day statistics bear this out. But perhaps a long time ago he got tired and gave Eve the job, the proper apparatus to produce and breasts to suckle the young, so that now all he has to do is sort the white sheep from the black, oil the pearly gates and clean the golden streets of His new city.

Anyway, snake or no snake, what we fail to see is: What did the apple have to do with getting Eve in the family way and why was God so angry when He found out? Perhaps he was jealous of Adam; or was he still dirt in His eyes? All of which is most ridiculous and asinine. Why would God create a man and woman and then become angry when they behaved as such? Also, how would the earth otherwise become populated? No populace—no saints and sinners; therefore no heaven—no hell; and God would be all alone in his universe.

CHAPTER 14

A Fool's Paradise

It often has been said that the Bible is the most contradictory book ever written and this is partially true when any attempt is made to analyze any of its apparent contradictions without a complete geneological knowledge of earth's history since plant and animal life began to flourish upon its surface.

In the foregoing paragraphs we have presented a rather humorous depiction of what might happen should any presupposed analysis be entered into without such knowledge and graphically illustrates the confusion which might arise from such an attempt.

The average Christian, however, is not interested in such analysis, nor does he possess sufficient knowledge for an intelligent introspection which would present a more factual picture. Moreover, the Christian religion, like all others, mandates a complete literal acceptance of its liturgy; and any and all translations or analysis being relegated strictly to the priesthood.

To the scientists, therefore, many of the stories and parables in the Bible are strictly myths and fantastic childlike stories which have arisen from the past ages of man's life upon the planet earth. By and large, the most controversial of all such stories are in the book of Genesis. The familiar story of man's creation and the Garden of Eden story are also contained within this book. These stories have achieved wide and questionable notoriety in both factions of science and religion, as well as from the average layman.

In defense of the Bible, however, it must be said that ridiculous and absurd as these stories may seem, there is often and usually a hidden interpretation which is in no wise understood by either science or religion.

In contradiction to the creation of man story in Genesis, the science of anthropology points out strong and conclusive evidence that man existed on this planet at least a million years ago; the skull of Pithecanthropus erectus, the Java man, is at least that old. The African skull found in 1958, called the Jinz skull, is at least 600,000 years old and was found along with several weapons which this man used in his daily battle for survival.

Forty or fifty thousand years ago, there were many bands and communities of people who lived or roamed throughout the various countries of Asia, Africa and Europe. They possessed weapons of stone and metal, used fire and cooked their food. More than 5,000 B.C., the Egyptians had a flourishing civilization along the banks of the Nile. 6,000 B.C. there were great civilizations throughout the Eastern and Oriental countries. This mass of archeological evidence is a strong contradiction to certain Christian beliefs.

The liturgy of Christianity points out a specific area in the Palestine region as the supposed place where the Garden of Eden once existed, 4,000 years B.C. Some strong Christian advocates have even pointed out the exact spot on the banks of the River Jordan, where God supposedly took the mud to make the first man. How fantastically ridiculous and absurd are these suppositions in the light of true knowledge of the historical anthropology of man; yet even this anthropological science is in no wise complete, nor does it tell of great civilizations that existed on this planet a million or more years ago and which have been completely wiped out by the great seismic, geographical changes of the earth, leaving no traces of these past civilizations.

Sufficient to say, however, that in the Bible and elsewhere, much pertinent information can be gathered on more recent civilizations, such as Lemuria and Atlantis. In fact we will turn to Genesis to obtain our first clue of the Lemurian civilization. Genesis states that the Lord made the earth in six days; these six days refer to six major cycles called in modern astronomy the recessional cycle which has an elapsed time period of 25,862 years. This refers to the mechanics of our solar system and our orbit around the sun. As we rotate once every 24 hours, we add up 365 days to make the theoretical point of completion of one complete cycle around the sun.

However, something is not quite right in this mathematical system. The earth is always so many hours and minutes late in arriving at this theoretical point of completion. This means, then, at the end of the 25,862 year period the earth has receded one complete cycle around the sun. This also means the earth has intercepted and bisected a great number of strong magnetic lines of force and their subsequent influences upon plant and animal life; and which retranslate this influence as cyclic epochs of time as they so concern plant and animal life, all of which idiomatically conforms to these various different influences exerted by these magnetic lines of force which are so interconnected with the Infinite Cosmogony, thus playing an important role in recreating some part in the infinite perspective as it concerns our planet earth.

Thus we have an understanding of the six days referred to in Genesis and which, when added up, take us back 156,000 or so years to the beginning of the Lemurian civilization; which actually means, that so

84

far as the Bible is concerned, begins its history of man at that date, and not on the banks of some river some 4,000 years B.C.

Moreover, the serpent in the Garden of Eden story is a parabolic reference to the science which was taught in the Lemurian age by the highly developed Adepts who came to this planet from the far-off planet Lemuria, at that time. The serpent symbolized the sine wave and just as it is taught in modern science, the Lemurian Masters tried to teach the aborigines of that time that all expressive or dynamic forms of life were actually sine wave configurations. This science, however, was not properly understood by the primitive mind, and the sine wave degenerated through the ages into the common symbology of the serpent; and the convolutions of some reptile along the ground was the nearest approach such primitive minds could conceive the manifestation of any dynamic realizations of energy forms.

Darwinism also presents strong controversial aspects to the story of the creation of man. Darwinism postulates a theorem of life as an evolutionary pattern which sprang from out the primeval ooze of some predawn earth epoch and, gradually, through adaptations to environmental changes, hereditary aspects, transmutations, etcetera, species were developed.

Here again Darwinism, just as any other biology, or anthropology and religion, fails to include the most important and dominant aspects in the creation and evolution of man, for this creation and subsequences of evolution must and always have originated in higher and "unknown" dimensions and the earth, like all other planets and planetary systems, presents only a surface or expressive element in which these creative and evolutionary patterns materialized in certain common reactive patterns of expression.

At this point of our introspection, it is now clearly indicated that there is much which can be and should be added, not only to Christianity and all other religions, but to all sciences as well; for in no instance do any of these sciences or religions include sufficient factual knowledge of these interdimensional factors which would give mankind a more comprehensive evaluation and understanding of his position to the Infinite.

The future will hold much in store for mankind upon this planet. In the beginning of space exploration, he has admitted the possibility of intelligent life on other planets and planetary systems. This, indirectly, is acknowledgment of the past when all races of man presently living are descendents of migrants from other planets; all races save one—the black man. The future will also hold a great emancipation from the fears and insecurities of earth life, particularly from fear of death, for with the knowledge of interdimensional relationship, man will see his pathway as a series of progressive evolutions into higher and more spiritual planes.

CHAPTER 15

The Face of Infinity

As you no doubt know by studying various historical configurations of religions and other documentaries which are contained in the various historical archives of the world, that they are concerned with man's spiritual progress into the Infinite. As has been explained previously to you, great cycles are manifest as infinite consciousness and man, in his search for a better position to orient himself into a happier and more compatible union with the Infinite, always seeks out and brings into his daily life, various and different configurations which have been termed religious or cultic observances. And so the histories of the world are filled with innumerable depictions of pageantries, fiestas and various other ritualistic observances which speak into the very subconscious fiber of each human being, and what he feels is some great and internal connection to the great Infinite.

The mystical and auric forces which surround him in great preponderant abundance, have always filled man with great awe, with a great sense of mysticism and with a failure to understand. In these things he has only tried to depict in his own way, what he believes should be the right thing to tender in his emotional reflexes to the great Infinite as he divides it into his consciousness; whether it is devised as a superficial form of consciousness of some god, as in the Christian religion or whether he adopts within his consciousness such configurations which involve hundreds or even thousands of deifications; all of which have their own particular specific point of equation in the emotional values of man's life on the planet earth.

And so man has lived, and lived again, and begat unto each generation and into the progeny of the following generations all of these things and many more; and thus, even the seasons of the year as they are woven in the fabrication of life are strange indeed. For while all of the content of man's life in the mental stance and lived in spiritual configurations which involved unknown and deistic forces which are beyond his comprehension and understanding, yet he refuses to acknowledge these dominant and spiritual influences into the reactions of his own personal interpretations to his fellow man.

He has always maintained his warlike attitudes, his lusts, his hates and the various tenacious and strenuous ways in which they wring the very essence of his life from the bowels of his mother earth. And so the seasons rise and fall and with them bring new interpretations, new configurations of some ruling deistic force which is so contrived in his own imagination, that it must indeed be the leaving off of some particular form and, with another, to again bring into succeeding days and months, some newer and different set of interpretations.

But how well it is put in Unarius works: that man always turns his face to Infinity and in the day by day turning, finds that there is a new interpretation so that man is never, in himself, static; nor are any of the other forces of the world he lives in static, but all maintain the same basic movement and relations to the Infinite. Even the atoms in your body are undergoing the same changes and in their own configurations of molecules and cell structures, they are being constantly replaced because the atoms themselves represent a form of consciousness of the Infinite.

And so into the future man will live and he will find the greatest of all messages which will be interpreted through his daily life. It is not the conflux of any one, or a group, or a number of seemingly external or mystical forces which reside in unknown dimensions about him but it is the way in which he interprets his own life from within his own mind. For in this interpretation does he so continually turn his face to the Infinite and in the turning does he incept into his own consciousness certain quantities of the Infinite Light which will develop and change his seemingly drab animal-like form of the man who is coming up from out of the more primitive developments of consciousness, into something which is indeed possessed of certain potentials which are as deistic as those which he has so contrived within his mind.

So my message to you dear ones as this season, calendrically speaking, takes a turn, is that you are only very vaguely conscious; that it is in the presupposition of the subconscious mind, vaguely reactionary in its pure sense; and that you must, to some degree, be mindful of the past, present and future in your small world in which the physical finds you.

Yes, there are times and sometimes there are places when there comes a great Light a great helping hand; a hand which has been strengthened with ages of wisdom and with living with one's self on the inner and with the higher denominators of spiritual integrity. And this great hand can—if one can reach out— by this hand be lifted and all of these things be made whole in the eyes of the Infinite. Yet these things cannot be so without a high degree of realization and the setting aside of the old.

Dear ones, you can indeed consider yourselves fortunate in contacting Unarius, yet it is in itself only more phases of your own personal realization; and you have earned what you are now realizing to a great degree, whether it be positive or negative expressions and whatever other manifestations that come are a direct orientation of a true understanding of love; and in that polarization and understanding of the facts of life as they should be understood, then all things are made equal in the eye of the Creator and you do indeed become a son of God.

So my message to you all is one simply that the new incoming season and each succeeding season will bring forth its own abundance and its own realizations in direct proportion to how well you live with the consciousness and that you can set aside permanently and forever, the small personal differences in your physical life. For these things only become a way in which you could destroy yourself; but with your face always toward the Light, your life can be a continuous revelation of manifestation of Truth and there may be many manifestations in the future, according to your individual efforts in the world about you. So therefore, keep your feet well placed on that spiraling pathway into the stars.

CHAPTER 16

False Prophets and Teachers

It has been said that the Bible is the greatest book which has ever been written; a readily admissible concession when certain considerations are made. Statistics show that as of today more than 800 million persons embrace Christianity, the cornerstone of which is the Bible. There is no available figure of the numbers of people who have embraced this same Christianity in the almost two thousand years of its existence. However, on the basis of pure analysis and upon certain important philosophical and psychological considerations, it is not conceded that the Bible is a book which can be considered a valid part of anyone's spiritual beliefs or life policies. For while the Bible is admittedly the greatest book, it must also be admitted that it is the greatest paradox, for there within its covers are presented two complete and opposite doctrines, and in conjunction with various supporting artifacts, historical configurations, the Bible is indeed much more than a paradox.

Perhaps the words of Spinoza, the great seventeenth century Dutch philosopher best describes the Bible. He said, "The Bible is filled with lies, lusts, fornications and murder and parts of it are not even fit to be read." For this and other similar statements Spinoza led the life of a hunted man and lived only by jumping from place to place, often narrowly escaping the minions of the church who, upon his capture, would gleefully have held one of their familiar "barbecues".

To the earnest seeker, therefore, who wishes to reconstruct a new life for himself, he must not be tempted to try to reconstruct such a new life from either excerpts from the Bible, or from any dogmatic church system which uses the Bible as its cornerstone. For history will reveal an odious fact: that it is the same Christianity which has been expressed and re-expressed in countless incidents, national and international wars, personal and mass hypocrisy and bigotry, murder, lust and fornication; all of which have been justified in the eyes of the bigots who wore the robes.

To further morally engage one's self in such past dispensations is obviously not feasible and would only lead the individual into a deeper morass of confusion and it's always attendant dire consequences of physical and mental disease. Nor should such constructive analysis or action be intimidated by personal recriminations or by the horrified looks and words of various life associates with whom the individual comes in contact. There are always those who would hurl the stigma of atheist; yes, even react in various acts of personal censorship which were obviously intended to ostracize such "drastic" conduct from the portals of their hallowed society.

However, dear reader, be of good cheer; you are taking the first steps which they, too, in the distant future must also take or face inevitable destruction by retrogressive action—the reversal of the dynamic principle of life—progression. If you are also deprived of the approbation of your fellowman, be not alarmed; there are many compensations which bestow beneficent blessings upon those who are endowed with enough courage and conviction to take these first steps; steps which will eventually lead away from the confusion, strife and despair of the material worlds, into higher and more expressive ways of life.

To better serve you, the student who is taking these first steps let us therefore analyze this Bible, knowing that in such an analytical preface you will be immediately confronted with and made aware of the great and almost hopeless tragedy of human emotion which is depicted in this book; hopeless, indeed, to all who would fill the vessel of their life with its vile and acrid contents.

Let us now first turn our attention to the Old Testament; here the process of analysis can be short and we will sever all moral implications as they so concern us personally. For such moral or spiritual implications would be based upon the literal acceptance, just as with hundreds of millions of people, of the old Chaldean god, Jehovah or Jahweh, a mythical god brought out of Ancient Chaldea by Father Abraham and perpetuated as the reigning deity in the framework of the Jewish and Christian religions.

Herein is the greatest of all paradoxes contained in the Bible. This old Chaldean Jehovah often displayed a violent temperament; he cavorted about the heavens indulging himself in various human-like emotions such as lust, greed, envy, jealousy, hate and fear. He quite frequently indulged himself in fornication with virgin maidens and sometimes let off sufficient steam to kill a few thousand people with whom he was displeased. Yes, he even shook down the walls and caused the sun to stand still so that those who were his humble servants could serve his purpose better in some mass murder. Strangely enough if any of his subjects indulged themselves in any of these vicissitudes even in a very small way, they would be condemned to everlasting hell or instantly destroyed.

It is this same god, Jehovah, which Jesus sought to destroy and eliminate from the minds of the people of Judea and yet, with this destruction of Jehovah, there would also obviously be the destruction of their religion which could not be tolerated by the rabbinical element or the Pharisees for this was their way of life. And so Jesus paid the price and died a religious malcontent upon a cross (so the Bible says), his only crime—teaching people a better way of life.

While the disparities between the Old and the New Testaments are quite obvious, there are also similar disparities in the New Testament and in particular to the Four Synoptic Gospels which form much of the hard core of Christianity. However, to best understand such conflicting disparities, we must realize that the beginnings of Christianity, as they were so conceived and started by Paul, were drawn from various sources. In almost all cases, however, there were few or no written records and the liturgy of the New Church was largely composed of various already existing religious observances and customs, such as the Mithraic cult which flourished in Greece at that time.

Contrary to general belief, Jesus did not have a formal designation of twelve apostles; this Apostolic designation came at a much later date, probably through St. Jerome, 400 A.D., who introduced the strongest and now existing Apostolic Acolyte. Incidentally, it is this same St. Jerome who is responsible for much of the obviously contradictory aspect in the New Testament, for St. Jerome, like Paul, was guilty of many outright embellishments and fabrications.

Since the Bible has been subject to translation into more than 1800 versions and languages, it is conceivable that, in translation, the original content has been sometimes lost or changed; however, the contents of the Bible and especially the New Testament, have been obviously changed and embellished far beyond that which would normally occur in a large number of translations.

Jesus offered a formal philosophy of life. Jesus

never spoke of God as the Lord or Jehovah, but always referred to God as "The Father", "It is the Father within which doeth all things" and again, "The Father and I are one and the same". As Jesus and the Father were one and the same, why then separate themselves as was depicted in the river Jordan baptismal scene and why would this same Jesus call himself His own Son and say that He was pleased with Himself?

There is, throughout the New Testament, an obvious attempt to introduce the old Jehovah wherever and whenever possible; the language frequently used refers to the Lord (Jehovah). There are other descriptions, too, of genealogical nature which would not have had any apparent interest or placement in the liturgy of Jesus. (Even the four Synoptic Books do not always conform or agree). Where then did all this material come from, this false coloration, devised methods of slanting, supernatural aura, liturgy? Certainly it was not contained in any written diaries or biographies which could have been used as base material for translation.

None of the so-called Apostles could read or write and only Luke, a physician and close associate of two of these Apostles, was literate. Some believed that he kept some kind of a diary; however, if this was so, it must have been destroyed after the first translation from Aramaic into Greek for the obvious reason that any future comparisons with this original text could be quite embarrassing. Therefore, it was with Paul, just as it was with St. Jerome and many others, the direct implication that this religion must be made strong enough with its dogma so that it could survive from one generation to the next. It was St. Jerome (later to be canonized), who attempted to rescue the Catholic church from almost certain oblivion by rewriting part of the Bible, especially the New Testament, so that they would institute new conformities which would give fresh power to the church and reinstate it as a ruling agent over masses of people.

For his efforts Jerome incurred the Pope's wrath and was banished to the Holy Land for two years; however, he was brought back in complete vindication, reinstated in the higher echelons of the church and lived to see his changes fully justified. There is more, much more, which could be discussed and analyzed in this same presentation of the historical beginning of Christianity. In previous texts we have discussed and pointed out how various old pagan customs were merged into the formation of this church, whether as a natural culmination of time and desire on the part of the people, or a deliberate attempt to proselyte other cults by their inclusion in the framework of the new church.

In the face of this great mass of evidential information, it seems incredible that hundreds of millions of otherwise fairly intelligent people could swallow this hocus-pocus, hook, line and sinker; that they have accepted without reserve, all the apparent derelictions, distortions, malfunctions, pandering, embellishments, emotional vicissitudes and superstitions, as part of the spiritual fabric of their lives.

And it is equally incredible that they not only hope for, but expect salvation to come out of this chaos of human derelictions. They have not stopped to consider that their future in the thousands of years to come, will depend upon how much constructive scientific information can be assimilated in the present and that nowhere within the tenets of the Christian liturgy is this information so contained, save only the few pearls of wisdom (spoken by Jesus), which somehow remain comparatively unadulterated. Yet, these pearls are insufficient and while they give us pertinent and valuable clues, no real constructive knowledge was given, for Jesus could not teach except in a manner best understood by those He taught. They would not have understood basic scientific elements which are the necessary ingredients of wisdom which will enable you to live in the distant future.

Gather ye not treasures on earth, but treasures of heaven.

Take heart therefore, dear reader, in moments of confusion or despair, or that you may feel intimidated to accept what seems to be an easier way; there are no easy ways! Only the acquisition and the usage of the necessary knowledge and wisdom will enable you to progressively advance into a higher way. This means tearing down and destroying so far as the reactive element is concerned, all of the past tenets of life which have been so valuable to you in their time.

Likewise, the future is always made from out such progressive cycles, each lasting thousands of years. This is the plan and purpose of the Infinite Mind, for in you, He has conceived another way in which He can live, not as an impersonal composition of all things, but as a separate living entity of consciousness which is capable of expressing all His attributes and propensities.

CHAPTER 17

Wanton Waste

In recent years many statistics have been compiled by various private and governmental research organizations. Some of these facts and figures are startling and alarming. Not the least of these statistics or figures which relate to a common human frailty is gambling. It is estimated that more than fifty million Americans gamble more than sixty billion dollars a year. These fifty odd million people can be said to be the more chronic type and do not include many millions more who take an occasional flyer into the gambling world.

These statistics immediately suggest a number of things. Sixty billion dollars is, in itself, a sizable sum of money and could go a long way toward assisting many very badly needed charitable efforts. Other statistics relating to human frailties are also quite startling and alarming. One hundred million or more Americans spend more than five billion dollars on cigarettes and associated tobacco habits.

There are more than ten million Americans acutely addicted to alcohol, plus an additional fifty or sixty million who drink occasionally or very modestly. The cost of these alcoholic beverages is also many billions of dollars per year. All these figures added up, would go a long way toward supporting various state governments as well as the Federal government and reduce taxes to a very low figure indeed. This, in turn, would create a much more abundant prosperity for all the one hundred seventy odd million Americans. There would be more money to buy the necessities of life and a few more luxuries.

Now, of course, it is not feasible or practical to ask all these various million American citizens to stop their gambling, smoking and drinking and, instead, put this misspent money directly into the hands of the various state and federal governments. They would immediately scream to high heaven, muttering various invectives and excusing their attitude by saying, "Everyone has a vice, I may as well have one too," or they might not consider their drinking and smoking a useless, demoralizing, physically weakening vice, (which it is), but say that it was necessary for their pleasure or, even for their health.

Gambling too would be personally supported by various lame-brained excuses; "I have to have some relaxation," etcetera. It has not occurred to these hundred odd million Americans that there is another substantial minority group living under their noses and with whom they associate daily, who do not gamble, drink, or smoke and who lead very happy normal lives; in fact, for the most part, this minority group lead far happier, healthier lives than do their smoke-filled, liquor-ridden, gambling neighbors.

Obviously this situation creates a great problem as suggested; that inasmuch as it is neither feasible nor practical to eliminate smoking and drinking, there should be another certain course of action pursued which would capitalize on these human frailties and inevitably tend to have an overall effect of not only lessening the evil of these useless proclivities, but would materially aid in bringing about a more abundant life for everyone.

During the 1920's, people lived under the Volstead Amendment, instigated and passed by the United

States government, to abolish liquor and the attendant evils of the notorious, demon, rum. Many who read these lines will remember the roaring 20's, a period of greater moral debauchery than has ever been witnessed in any other historical decade. People who would otherwise never have touched a drop, were drawn into the net of moral decadency by the reverse psychology instituted by the act of prohibition.

Everyone knows that one way to get a child to do something is to prohibit him from doing it. As common childhood traits and patterns are so formed in the early years, they are of course the dominant patterns of reflex action always used by the adult in later life. In other words, in this sense then, adults are still children. Bearing these psychological factors in mind, it is easy to see that illegal gambling in the United States has the same effect as prohibited drinking. The equations here are exactly similar except one is gambling and the other is liquor.

Moreover, it is well known that such illegal or prohibited activity, such as gambling, creates a certain very demoralizing effect in the moral attitude of any person who knowingly breaks the law in indulging himself in one or more of the various prohibited, illegal gambling activities. In any given length of time, this person will gradually lose all sense of respect for law, order and decency in any and all other forms and manifestations of human conduct and their associated governing laws.

In line with this reasoning, coupled together with some other existing facts and figures, leads us to the inevitable conclusion that gambling should be legalized in all states of the Union. Why not then, take advantage of this human frailty and turn it into some good account?

Right here, the author would like to say that he does not believe in gambling; he belongs to that minority group of many millions of Americans who also do not believe or participate in such activities; nor has he ever contributed a single dollar to the countless billions which have been poured into the pockets of the organized underworld organizations who foster these various gambling activities. Horse racing, cards, lotteries, dice, roulette, bingo, are some of the commonly known forms.

At this time, we must point out that at least one state in the Union, specifically Nevada, has legalized gambling and this state has derived great financial benefits from taxes levied on the gambling activities in that state. As a matter of fact, Nevada has lower state taxes than any state in the Union. Also, the little kingdom of Monaco, ruled over by Prince Rainier and Princess Grace (Kelly), is entirely tax free; the government being supported entirely from the taxes levied on its gambling salons. And all the citizens of Monaco lead happy lives, entirely freed from the odious burden of paying heavy taxes, filling out income tax returns, plus the endless red tape involvements.

It should also be noted that under the conditions of legalized gambling, strong governmental control can be exercised and the so-called clean form of gambling maintained. In a sense, the government has already been so established in the tobacco and liquor industries, for here the federal and various state governments derive great financial support from taxes levied on these two specific vices. Then, why not be practical and realistic in respect to gambling?

The author is not alone in his advocation of legalized gambling. Thousands of public-minded citizens comprising elements which belong to various educational, medical and psychiatric groups, lawyers and teachers have been very outspoken in this cause to promote legalized gambling.

Many believe, just as does the author, that such legalized gambling would very definitely tend to curb and eventually eliminate organized gangsterism as it now exists in this country. At one time, a certain well-known figure named McAfee ran more than one thousand houses of prostitution in the Los Angeles (California) area, along with various sundry and associated vices, including gambling. Finally the irate citizens elected a new mayor and city government, then McAfee with his protector, Shaw, moved to Las Vegas, Nevada, where he now conducts and controls a large part of the gambling in that city; and in this control, under state supervision, he has been forced to lead a much cleaner and more decent life. Moreover, all his clients are now not breaking the law and there is no subsequent demoralizing effect.

The gist of this analysis simply boils down to this: It is much more realistic and far easier to cope with a dangerous situation when it is out in the open and you can compensate for all factors involved. A tiger in a zoo is a harmless animal; he is under complete control and observation at all times but this same tiger in the jungle is a far different matter.

Therefore, let us face the problem of equating certain human frailties in a more realistic manner. Like the old madrigal of the mice who belled the cat, let us also put a bell around the neck of this most ferocious animal, "gambling". At least the decent citizens will know where he is and what he is doing and, if need be, restrictions can be speedily placed upon him.

CHAPTER 18

The Dishonor System

It might be well to note that even as our article on gambling was being edited for the press, the April 27th date carried in numerous syndicated newspapers and other news sources the following news items to wit, that the United States Bureau of Internal Revenue was sending forth from Washington, a certain especially trained group of tax men. Their purpose was to crack down on the various gamblers and gambling syndicates throughout the country for failure to pay their annual $50.00 yearly income license fee which is demanded by our Government.

It is indeed a strange paradox that, while gambling is illegal in all states except one, that there seems to be no way of bringing these various gambling racketeers to their just deserts and stamping out this national evil. This is very reminiscent of the era of prohibition when the notorious king of criminals, Al Capone, controlled a large gang of racketeers in the northeastern states of our country. Besides bootlegging and various other associated crimes, Capone was believed to be responsible for at least 400 murders; yet the United States Government could not prosecute or convict this arch-criminal, except on his failure to pay income tax on the hundreds of millions of dollars he had collected illegally.

While we have specifically mentioned Nevada as a

state which somehow has exempted itself from certain specific Federal statutes supposed to control gambling, this situation is not as unique as the small municipality of Gardena, which lies a few miles out, in the southwestern area of Los Angeles, California. Within its city limits, Gardena has legalized poker playing, bingo and other associated forms of gambling in complete contradiction to State and Federal laws and, in this respect, has virtually become another kingdom of Monaco.

It is small wonder indeed that the average American has sort of an indifferent contempt for the many thousands of laws and the law enforcement agencies. The average citizen, too, is known to bilk his government out of every possible cent of income tax. In view of the vastly preponderant and almost ineffective system of legislative, judicial and law enforcement agencies, the average citizen may be partially justified in his actions, for it is quite well known that Mr. John Q. Citizen pays a much higher income tax than did the serfs in the baronial estates in the Middle Ages. There is indeed small wonder that the average child grows up into adulthood with the same indifferent disrespect and this universal disrespect is being nationally expressed in the figures—percentage-wise—of the eligible voters of this country; the percentage being about 40 percent, whereas in European countries such as Italy and France, the percent-age of voting eligible voters is over 90 percent. Perhaps this low 40 percent figure also speaks of a certain disrespect or contempt for the leaders of the political parties and the various candidates they nominate for the high governmental positions.

So far as gambling is concerned, however, we have expressed the opinion that it would be much better to make gambling nationally legal and place it under strict governmental control, tax it a good healthy 33 percent, as they do in Nevada, and use the vast tax proceeds to help support our over preponderant and extremely ineffectual, inefficient, conflicting government.

In the words of the immortal Webster, "If these be treasonable words, then make the most of them," for they are words expressed universally by many millions of Americans who, just as we, are watching the rotten corruption of vice, graft and deceit, creeping into the very moral framework and tissue of this great country.

It is also well to mention, at the same time the Internal Revenue men were sent out upon their appointed task, another form of vice and corruption was being aired and exposed to the public.

Through the medium of television, in a one-hour show viewed coast to coast, this racket was dramatically exposed in all its horrible implications. This is the racket known as the "Dishonor System". Throughout the various colleges and universities in the United States, there are certain groups of racketeers operating almost legally and in open and apparent unconcern. They are certain specific groups of organized ghost writers who openly advertise on campus and college bulletin boards. They will underwrite, for a fee, the various test papers and theses which the college student periodically turns in to his professors.

In effect, this means that many college students have gone and are going through college, acting merely as puppets. Their sole purpose was to acquire a diploma and degree without actually studying for and acquiring this coveted degree in the normal manner.

The vicious demoralizing effect of this crime is readily apparent, for it strikes into the very heart and roots of the moral fiber of this great country and its educational system. The future of this country will depend to a large degree upon the effectiveness of these educational systems and, while they are presently somewhat inefficient, they are at least one of the sustaining bastions of this civilization. Fortunately, as of this time, only a comparatively small percentage of the students have availed themselves of these services and as it has become nationally recognized. No doubt more suitable measures will be taken to suppress this immoral activity. However, should this come about, no doubt ghost writing will go underground and the student who engages a ghost writer to write up his various test and thesis papers will be reduced to a common criminal. History has proven the ineffectiveness of suppression. The era of prohibition is a classical example as well as our present and widespread national gambling. The answers to these various moral problems therefore, do not lie within the dimension of legal suppression and law enforcement; they must become educational factors, sustained throughout the life of any individual from cradle to grave.

The people of this country would have to publicly support any and all campaigns of voluntary suppression of instigating sources. For instance, more than 20 million children are exposed daily in their own homes to thousands of vivid and shocking portrayals of murder, vice, crime and adultery which ride roughshod across television screens; or they may go to the movies and see law, order and decency flaunted. Criminals and organized crime, prostitution and vice have become part of the growing-up life of every American child.

Small wonder that we have the many and ever-increasing rates of incidence in juvenile delinquency, dope addiction, murder, sex and the ever-increasing divorce rate; in short, all lending power to that great invisible finger which is writing its prophecy of doom upon the walls of our civilization.

CHAPTER 19

Terrifying Television

In various articles published by Unarius, certain inferences have been made about present existing signs of a decadent age and the author of these articles does not wish to be classified as one of the currently existing doom-mongers or crepe-hangers, who go about deploring the general state of things and prophesying an early end of the earth.

On the premise that any constructive and progressive evolution made by any culture or civilization is, by necessity, composed of many constructive factors such as a healthy environment for all citizens, adequate laws and enforcement to govern various intemperances and above all, a keen and alert attitude by citizens and leaders alike; for any unhealthy trends could, if they remained unchecked, undermine the moral fiber of this nation, even causing its eventual collapse and disintegration.

It has been observed by almost everyone that the better things in life are obtained only at great effort and self-determination; and they are held only by an equally great effort. At the present time there are many destructive and corrosive trends currently expressing themselves, some very flagrantly, seemingly without corrective opposition. At least one or two of these trends could be the acid which will eat away the bastions of our civilization and, when combined with a number of others which are presently flourishing, then surely we, the citizens of today have doomed the tomorrow by our indifferent attitude.

By far, the greatest single corrosive trend which is making a tremendous contribution to a decadent age is the mounting rate of incidence of juvenile delinquency among the younger generation. Without a doubt, the greatest single contributing factor to juvenile delinquency is the television set, one or more of which are found in almost every home. These said television sets are flooding the American homes with murder, sadism, prostitution, gambling and other such various vile panderings of debased human emotions.

The author is not alone or singularly aware of this national crisis which has been mounting in tempo for the past twenty years. Educators, doctors, psychiatrists and various executive, preventive and judicial branches of our national, state and city governments are keenly aware of this problem and which, in the general consensus of opinions, have found that the various crime programs to which the children are exposed, have warped their personalities, made them indifferent to human suffering, unsympathetic, uncooperative and imbued with a contempt for law, order and decency.

May we repeat a few statistics currently published by various census and research groups as well as law enforcement agencies. J. Edgar Hoover stated in two syndicated articles that 51 percent of the crimes committed in the United States are by the American youth before he reaches the age twenty-one. Over 31 percent of all dope addiction is found in the adolescent— teenage group. These are but a few of the alarming statistics which point toward the down-hill trail.

*These statistics quoted were as of 1960. (Now at the turn of the century the figures are even more appalling.)

Let us find how television has been the chief contributing cause toward juvenile delinquency. In 1952, the American Medical Association, in their medical journal, published an editorial which gave definite warning at that time, of the trend of juvenile delinquency which was being created by the crime programs beamed at our children. The 25 million youngsters who view television daily, see a total of 25,000 million hours of broadcasting devoted to crime programs yearly.

It is very significant to note that since the publication of the editorial in the medical journal, there has been an 800 percent increase in juvenile delinquency up to 1958. This increase is in direct ratio with an 800 percent increase in the number of child viewers of these crime programs for which various sponsors spend over 500 billion dollars yearly. This sum does not include other kinds of shows which do not show crime.

If a child starts at the age of 6 to view television, by the time he reaches the age of 18, he will have seen 17,000 people killed in violent action as they are portrayed in more than 10,000 yearly crime shows. These figures, staggering as they are, cannot be fully appreciated unless we also understand the tremendous psychological impact which this constant and never-ending portrayal of death, vice and prostitution has upon the mind and subconscious of the growing child.

While the broadcasters claim there are no ill effects from these shows, the grim evidence is there. These various broadcasters have openly declared their firm intentions to uphold the highest moral standards in their program material; yet recent surveys made in different cities show that these same broadcasters give as much as 400 hours a month to crime shows. Moreover, not only are these Westerns and other types of crime shows becoming more violent, they are purposely beamed at such times when the youngsters have access to the television set.

It has been found in these same surveys that some stations, during the 7 to 11 P.M. period, run as many as four consecutive hours of crime during the Friday, Saturday and Sunday weekend period; and some of the weeknights are almost as bad. Sponsors and broadcasters alike, have unashamedly admitted this fact. In these various crime shows, particularly the Westerns, law, order and justice are flouted. The criminal is made a hero; his exploits only partially tempered by an equally great killer, the peace officer.

These peace officers are very often seen in saloons gulping down hard whiskey, gambling with the criminals and female prostitutes. In short, there is often very little difference between the criminal and peace officer, save the badge. Women, too, come in for their share of distortions; the good and virtuous housewife is most often seen, worn and haggard, bending over a washtub or chopping wood while the prostitutes live a life of glittering opulence in the local saloon.

It would be difficult to imagine the turmoil which goes on in the childish mind when he attempts to justify and compromise his approach to understanding the new life about him, for in these tender years, everything seen and heard by the child always becomes some part of his ratio of comparisons. It is therefore easy to see that such a child who spends several hours daily viewing these vile intemperances will inevitably grow up devoid of certain moral values and will have much less strength to back them up.

The results of this terrible juvenile delinquency is a matter of national concern; and every daily newspaper carries one or more incidents wherein some juvenile has started a one-man crime wave. Two such recent incidents—one 17-year-old boy committed nine murders before he was stopped; another 14-year-old boy (Whitney), hitch-hiked from Los Angeles, California to Florida and killed seven people on the way. Another typical example of juvenile delinquency was found in New York city, during 1959; the teen-age gangsters killed more than 20 people in that city.

Nor do all of the full implications of this juvenile delinquency reach the public eye or ear. Various juvenile centers, maternity wards and other such associated places should be visited to find a more complete picture of this problem. Watch the teen-age gangsters and hoodlums racing up and down the public streets in their souped-up hot-rods, often beating up and even killing defenseless people, sometimes for nothing more than the vicarious thrill, following the pattern of some hoodlum gangster or Western idol portrayed on the television screen which they saw in their previous years.

Movies, too, come in for a fair share of this nefarious criminal practice and most movie houses in the larger cities and suburbs have become veritable child and teen-age jungles where, during the long double and triple feature programs, children of all levels of life associate promiscuously, learning bad habits, perverted sex practices and marijuana smoking from various profligates from the lower seamy side of the city. These are all definite indications of a disastrous climax to this world of tomorrow; for as the twig is bent, so the tree grows.

In one recent survey, the children were asked what vocation they would choose; only 6 percent chose to be scientists. When asked why, they said scientists were queer, freaks, monsters, weirdos; and no wonder, after constantly seeing Frankenstein and Dr. Jekel and Mr. Hyde and other mad scientists. The children have little longing to become one of these hard working, patient men and women who have contributed more to our society than any other single faction.

Worse, still, when compared to our competitive nation Russia, where more than 20 percent of the children start out to be scientists (some estimates say 50 percent), for in Russia the scientist is usually a public hero, is better paid and lives better than any other citizen; and we are depending, in one sense, upon survival, from our scientific technocracy in competition with Russia.

This, then, is the trend of today which becomes the fact of tomorrow and the facts of tomorrow will indeed be grim, if these trends of today are not checked. In the common conduct of human ethics, the cause of law enforcement is never fully justified; two wrongs never make a right, for law enforcement involves not only penal and capital punishment, but sometimes the act of apprehending is one of violence and death.

The only sane and logical solution to any national problem lies in the pure dimension of suitable and correct educational values propagated in an atmosphere and environment which is sterile of all criminal malpractices and any attendant seductive influences. Other various and adjunctive educational elements have been discussed in various articles of Unarius and, if all of these factors and elements are brought together, and if so vigorously pursued in the next ten generations they would place this nation, culturally speaking, far in advance of any nation past or present.

It is interesting to note that during the recent months 1959-60), national attention was focused on Washington, D.C., where a Senate Investigations Committee was probing into the graft and corruption going on in various television quiz shows aired throughout the country. Various sponsors and producers of these quiz shows were subpoenaed before the Board and while results were rather vague to the general public, yet certain new rulings were instigated. Disc Jockeys, too, came in for their share of unfavorable notoriety; the word 'payola' became a household term.

Two officials also resigned, one a Mr. Mac, who headed the Federal Communications Commission and the other, the Columbia Broadcasting System president. This investigation effort, however, can be considered very commendable and shows what can be done when public interest is sufficiently aroused.

Today millions of parents and various other groups of individuals interested in public welfare are hoping and praying that the spotlight will be turned upon the television crime shows. So long as the general public remains apathetic to this great need, criminals of all kinds will continue to ride roughshod through American homes, shooting and killing as they go and we will continue to have a rise in our juvenile delinquency problem.

In 1959, two bills were presented to Congress which would authorize several million dollars to be used in investigating and curtailing the juvenile delinquency problem. How well it would be if our law-makers did the first and most obvious thing: clean up the crime wave on television and return it to its rightful position as one of the greatest entertainment and educational mediums of these times. Until that day arrives, however, much can be done to alleviate this situation; a national boycott imposed against crime shows by parents would very quickly achieve the desired results, for as the ratings on these shows dropped, sponsors would no longer support them and they would be withdrawn.

Also a flood of letters to Congress from millions of angered constituents would also speed the day of recovery from this ghastly condition. For, if the future generations are to live happily in their future world, we, the people of the present must use every means at our command to curtail and obliterate this and all other unwholesome trends to make sure the basic foundation upon which the future will be built, has not been, and shall not be weakened.

CHAPTER 20

Adding Addictions

It is inevitable that sooner or later the searching eye of Unarius would be focused upon another common human frailty, specifically, drug addiction. This term immediately suggests to the reader pictures of vile opium dens where poor human derelicts smoke themselves to death. It will therefore be surprising and startling for the reader to learn that the greater majority of the people on the planet earth are drug addicts; in fact, your friends, relatives and neighbors —even you, yourself, may be a drug addict!

Within the well-defined dimension of drug addiction, the definition of drug addiction is: the use of any chemical or chemical compound, taken internally in one manner or another, singularly or combined with foods, vapors, liquids, mendicants, the said chemicals or chemical compounds having a definite and known effect upon the physical anatomy and its mental functions and reactions, the said and specific use of these chemicals being taken beyond a certain norm.

This norm is only the occasional usage of such chemicals as a reactive or medicinal agent, temporarily used to combat or relieve certain specified human ailments and when correction occurs, the use of the chemical or drug is discontinued. In this very wide and broadly defined dimension, drug addiction can therefore be said to include even the common and universal usages of coffee and tea. A cup of coffee contains two and one-half grains of caffeine.

Caffeine is a heart stimulant and has been used on many an occasion by doctors who interject it intravenously to keep a patient alive sufficiently long enough to sign a will or a confession. Aspirin compound and seltzer can also be considered in this respect—chemicals used in a common form of addiction. Many people are known to consume great quantities of coffee, aspirin or seltzer in an attempt to relieve symptomatic psychic pressure or various nervous conditions.

Looking at the people living in various countries throughout the world, we find natives in South America, India and Eastern Archipelagos, chewing coca leaves taken from a tropical shrub which grows in these countries—the same leaves from which the notorious cocaine is distilled.

In China, the use of opium is very universal; in some cities an estimated 75 percent of the population are either mild or heavy addicts. Opium is derived from the poppy plant, shortly after the blooms have faded; a silver scraper is used to scrape the juice from the seed-pod. This juice is collected and boiled down to a thick black, gummy substance and from this vile brew, morphine and heroin are extracted which are used extensively in Europe and America.

In India, Borneo, Thailand, especially, milder forms of drug addiction include chewing betel nut. In the near East, Greece, Asia Minor, Egypt, etcetera, hashish or hemp smoking is a common form of addiction. It was a cup of distilled hemp juice which Socrates drank in that famous historical episode known to almost all literate people of the world; for hemp, like other alkaloids and alkaloid derivatives is a deadly poison if taken in "large doses".

If you were to extract the caffeine from one cup of coffee and inject it intravenously, you would most likely die from a serious heart thrombosis in a few minutes time. Fortunately for everyone who drinks coffee, caffeine is assimilated very slowly when taken internally and under this "controlled" condition, the body can absorb large quantities of caffeine without serious results.

Loosely speaking, almost all such types of narcotics or dope are derived from various forms of vegetation which include the popular and universally used tobacco. Nicotine is also an alkaloid; its effect on the heart and nervous system, however, is opposite from that of caffeine, acting as a depressant. Tea contains an alkaloid known as theine, also a stimulant.

However, we cannot neglect other chemicals absorbed into the human system when we drink coffee and tea. One of these is tannic acid, the same chemical used to tan leather and which is a part of that complex chemical structure known as creolin or vegetable coal tars. Within the realm of these creolin compounds, the scientist has been able to extract and synthesize more than 10,000 different chemical compounds, dyes, drugs, fibers such as nylon and dacron. These also include the phenols which are used to manufacture the various barbiturates or sleeping pills, commonly referred to as goof balls, bennies and pep pills. Seconal is a very popular, wide-spread sleeping or deadening agent, prescribed by doctors and bootlegged by druggists and is used by a certain group of teen-agers who practice their own type of addiction.

In the past few years public attention has been focused upon a number of deaths which consistently occurred from over-dosages of sleeping pills and which could not be classified as suicides. As in the case of all types of addictions, a form of dependency is built up starting from a small dose, then an ever increasingly larger dose is demanded by the victim as the mind and body builds up a certain resistance against the drug. The use of any and all such chemicals in the human system either as stimulants or depressants always has a two-way action.

In the case of a depressant such as in the one of tobacco, the body is temporarily depressed or stunned by the introduction of large quantities of various chemicals. The smoker seems to feel he is relieved; however, as the body begins to free itself and cast off these various chemicals, it bounces, so to speak, in the opposite direction; nerves and tissues are slightly more sensitized than they were before the introduction of the chemicals. This immediately demands another dose in the effort to relieve this aggravated condition; and, so the pattern goes. The poor victim is now struggling between what he knows is the right thing to do—complete discontinuance—and the continued and ever-increasing dosages.

This is the common conflict fought by every tobacco smoker. The same holds true to some extent for the tea and coffee drinker. This conflict also goes on with the heroin addict as well as the sleeping pill addict. In an effort to get a nights sleep, he takes one pill; then two or three; then some night, in an overdosed condition and still not sleeping, his hands will grope for the bottle and not being able to remember or even count correctly, he will take that fatal overdose. This is what happened to Amie Semple McPherson, the famous Evangelist and it has happened to many thousands of people before and after that episode.

Proceeding now into more specific areas of what can be called the heavy or major addictions, let us first consider the present national problem of dope addiction as it concerns the use of heroin and which is especially prevalent among teenagers of this country. The actual number of addicts in this category is not known; however, it is believed to run into several million. There are 240,000 known and registered addicts in the United States, in contrast with the British Isles which have a registered number of 3,000. These statistics, incidentally, are used in a presently existing, hot controversy between two factions of law enforcement agencies who are trying to control this narcotic addiction (as of 1960).

In Britain, dope addicts can legally buy, in the drug store, the necessary daily dosages with a doctor's prescription. In this country, the addict must become a criminal and must buy from an undercover agent. Moreover, while the price is very nominal in Britain, it is enormously high in this country. Any addict who is thoroughly "hooked" on heroin, is forced to take three or four shots a day; this means he will pay out from $75.00 to $200.00 a day in cold, hard cash to enable him to sustain his habit. This, of course, means he cannot earn enough holding down an ordinary job; he is forced to go out and rob, steal and murder in order to obtain his daily supply.

In the case of a female addict, she is usually forced into a life of prostitution to support her addiction, whereas, it is claimed by the proponents of legalized drug selling that these great evils would be automatically done away with—the dope peddler and the attendant crime and prostitution would vanish—when the addict could walk into the drug store and purchase his daily supply from his wages he had earned.

Of course, in the severe cases of addiction, the victim is unable to hold down a regular job; he is unreliable and unstable and no doubt these people would become charity cases. In any event, the national problem as it concerns dope addiction in this direction is indeed grave and extremely complex; at the present time, there is no clear or concise plan of control or elimination and for the time being, it is quite likely to dominate the list of public menaces which are contributing to the decadency of these times.

At this point it would be well to focus our attention

upon the number one popular public drug addiction —specifically, the use of tobacco, for in this category, we find that it exceeds by far all other types and forms of addictions. The seriousness of this addiction cannot fully be estimated because of the slower and more insidious, long-range effect smoking has on the human anatomy. In the use of heroin, the effect is quick and very noticeable but in tobacco addiction, the effects are more difficult to measure and to establish as the contributing basic factor of certain types of human malfunctions. Every smoker knows from personal experience that his habit is not good for him; most smokers have proven this by temporarily quitting and finding a new measure of health in those few weeks when they abstained from their habit.

Specifically, let us now look into such areas of physical conditions which are called cancer and general toxemia. General toxemia is a form of conjunctivitis which noticeably shortens the life of tobacco users. Since 1950, much research work has been done in this field and particularly with cancer. In the early 1950's general medical practice had noted and recorded an 800 percent increase in lung cancer, especially among males. In attempting to probe into various causations, researchers discovered many interesting facts, all directly connected to smoking.

For instance, in 1954, Dr. Cameron at Berkeley University, then president of the American Medical Association, made a national report on the findings of his staff, who worked with 250,000 people over a period of several years. In this report, a most astounding and significant fact was revealed: tobacco smokers over the age of 50 years shortened their life expectancy by as much as 60 percent. In another report, the late Dr. Raymond Pearl, a famous physician from the Mayo Clinic in Rochester, Minnesota, stated that a woman who smokes a pack of cigarettes per day, ages her face an additional year in every five years; yet these same millions of women spend several hundred billion dollars yearly buying cosmetics and going to beauty parlors.

Numerous reports have been made by various research organizations on lung cancer and they have all compiled an overwhelming mass of evidence which points its finger at tobacco smoking as the guilty agent and chief contributing factor in the 800 percent rise of lung cancer. From this point on, a never-ending stream of facts, figures and findings could be introduced and yet in all of these statistics very little mention has been given to what is perhaps the worst of all effects incurred in this popular addiction—specifically, carbon monoxide poisoning.

The National Safety Council is constantly issuing warnings about defective automobile mufflers and heaters in homes, which yearly cause several thousands of deaths but no one as yet has issued a warning to the smoker who is, in effect, placing his mouth over the exhaust pipe of an automobile every time he lights a cigarette. Many laboratory tests have proven that smoking one cigarette and inhaling a number of puffs will increase carbon monoxide precipitation in the blood stream by two and one-half percent.

In the early 1950's, research was carried on by a medical board of doctors in Los Angeles, California, who were seeking an answer to what effect smog had on the human system. These doctors found that in congested, downtown areas, carbon monoxide precipitation averaged 6 percent above normal with the nonsmokers, whereas their fellow workers who were heavy smokers averaged as much as 12 percent—and 13 percent is considered fatal.

In short then, the average smoker carries more than twice as much carbon monoxide in his blood as does the nonsmoker. One of these Los Angeles doctors said, "Inhaling one drag from a cigarette is more than equivalent to inhaling dense smog for 24 hours." Various other private and national researchers have revealed the fact that the smoker is from 10 to 20 percent below par, both in his general physical metabolism and his mental reactions.

It is estimated there are over 200,000 Americans who wander from day to day, in and out of doctors offices and clinics, all of them half sick and trying to get help and relief from various imaginary complaints and, in most cases, physical checkups have revealed that there was nothing wrong with them except that they smoked two or more packages of cigarettes a day.

Before the beginning of the 20th century, missionaries and other people going into the South Sea Islands were sometimes killed and eaten by cannibals. These cannibals, however, would never eat the flesh of a man who smoked because they would become violently ill, just as does a boy who smokes his father's pipe or cigar for the first time.

It has been found in numerous laboratory experiments that the nicotine extracted from one cigarette can kill a good sized dog. It is this same nicotine which is used in garden insecticides to kill bugs. Recently two French doctors and chemical researchers isolated certain chemicals in tobacco which, when used on rats, mice and rabbits, produced cancer. In view of this great overwhelming mass of evidence, it is indeed strange that people go right on smoking. Tobacco companies have directly admitted the caustic effect of smoking by putting filters on their cigarettes. How silly this is. While every smoker knows and admits the harmful effect of this habit, he will buy the filter cigarettes even though this habit must be sustained by the narcotic effect of tobacco upon his system.

In other words, if the filter removed all toxic elements and drugs from the smoke, there would be

121

no smoke left, only water vapor. Tobacco companies know that when filters were first introduced, smokers did not like them because the tobacco used was too mild; by the time the smoke got through the filter, the smoker did not get his accustomed 'kick' or reaction; so the tobacco people counteracted this by using strong, cheap tobacco which, when drawn through a filter, was strong enough to give the smoker his craved reaction. Tobacco companies now pay more for cheap, strong tobacco than they formerly did for the more mild, bland blends.

Up until this point we have discussed only the chemical or autointoxicant effect of tobacco on the system. There are actually 234 known chemical poisons in a cigarette including furfurol, the deadliest poison in the medical pharmacopoeia. The effect of smoking in the popular form of drug addiction is not confined to chemical reactions. There is also a psychological reaction which is quite destructive to the moral fiber of the smoker. This demoralizing action hinges upon an escape mechanism which was formed from the many complexes, compounded from various insecurities, deflations and guilts which the smoker has incurred in his lifetime from birth.

When a baby is born into the world, his first great fear or insecurity is hunger. As the nipple is pushed into his mouth, he quickly learns that this gnawing hunger-fear is relieved; this forms an association complex with various other kinds of fears and pains with which he comes in contact in his new environment. And so, to the infant, the nipple becomes the panacea of all ills and troubles.

Just about the time he becomes somewhat satisfied with this regular tranquilizing effect the nipple has upon him, his parents suddenly take it away from him and he suffers his first shock and induces his first neurosis. From then on, this neurosis will remain with him—throughout his life. It will, of course, be compounded in later years with other neuroses. Now the child is emotionally disturbed by having been weaned, so he takes to various defense and escape mechanisms. He eats dirt, worms, flies and mud-pies, or he may have tantrums, hold his breath and turn blue, or he may have nightmares and scream all night.

When he goes to school, he will chew up his pencils and eat his wax crayons. As the list of various shocks, deflations and fears are lived through, he adds to this general neurosis. To some extent these may be partially dissipated, more so in some children than in others, depending of course upon many factors.

By the time he reaches adolescence, he may be quite neurotic and he, like other teen-agers, seeks various means of escape from this neurosis such as are now currently expressed. The be-bop, rock-and-roll music, the strenuous forms of dancing; jitterbug, etcetera and these complexes and escape mechanisms are always greatly complicated by the newly acquired dimension of sex. The various queer, weird attitudes of teen-agers can therefore be partially justified; in fact he would be abnormal if he did not seek a means of escape. We can also now easily see where, under more extreme conditions, the teen-ager will take more drastic means of escape, starting to smoke not only tobacco but another one of the more popular addictions—smoking marijuana.

(Smoking therefore can be considered "grown-up" nipple-nursing and thumb-sucking.)

At this point we must not neglect the factor of cost of the national drug addiction to tobacco. Tobacco consumption is 11½ pounds per capita, which costs the smokers over five billion dollars. This figure does not include another almost one-third percent of the one billion dollar national fire bill, and these national fire losses are small in comparison to the hundreds of billions of dollars lost in forest fires, the chief contributing cause being the careless smoker. We must also be mindful of the ten thousand men, women and children who die each year, directly or indirectly, from careless smoking habits.

The effect of marijuana on the system is quite similar to many other opiates; it has an accelerating, freeing effect on the mental perspective. It also sexually effects the user. Many a teen-age girl has lost her virtue after smoking her first "reefer", for in her semi-drugged condition, all moral values and issues have no meaning and her sexual mechanism has been over-sensitized.

It is estimated by some researchers that in all high schools throughout the country nearly all students, at one time or another, smoke one or more "reefers", for the weed from which marijuana is made can be grown in flowerpots in a window or in anyone's backyard. Marijuana has been found growing in many American cities. One man in Los Angeles, California, actually grew and cultivated a hedge grown from marijuana plants, not knowing what the weed was; the seed having been given to him by an acquaintance who was a "pusher".

Directly or indirectly, all of the 51 percent of the total crimes committed in the United States by teenagers were done when these boys and girls were under the influence of marijuana, goof-balls, barbiturates or heroin. Therefore the effect on the general public from drug addiction cannot be fully estimated. The comparatively milder forms such as tea and coffee, aspirins, seltzers and such can be disregarded in view of the greater and more drastic effect that the heavier addictions have upon the general public's moral and physical health.

Alcoholism, too, is one more of the serious and flagrant types of addiction, for alcohol is an anesthesia, deadening mental and physical reactions. It also produces several serious physical effects, such as cirrhosis of the liver. It is estimated that there are about ten million acute alcoholics in the United States. These are people who are partially or totally drunk all the time. There are at least another sixty million or more who drink occasionally, or a cocktail or two a day and only an occasional drunken spree. This type of addiction, in itself, is serious enough but is small in comparison to the general public addiction of smoking which involves at least one hundred million Americans. Because smoking is much more insidious in its effects and less noticed over a long time period, tobacco should then be labeled "public enemy number one"; and the government as they do in Russia, should enter into a direct campaign to encourage voluntary suppression and discourage its use.

In the same psychological vein, smoking and drug usages of various kinds can be considered a masochistic perversion; there is always a direct or indirect subconscious reaction connected with the sexual mechanism which occurs when any foreign substance (or thing), is introduced into the human anatomy and which cannot be considered normal, such as eating or breathing.

Smoking, therefore, demands a double indemnity; the smoker pays not only in his general health but is continuously destroying his moral character by this constantly repeated, subconscious perversion; i.e., he knows that it is wrong and gets a vicarious kick out of doing wrong as a means of getting even for various ego deflations which he has suffered; or he may be punishing himself (self flagellation) for his various failures and weaknesses. Flagellation is a known sex perversion.

Complete analysis is difficult and complicated but, as a whole, such devices as smoking should be considered as a constant source of stimulation for these various destructive subconscious mechanisms.

Liquors and tobaccos do produce large governmental revenues therefore these should be increased. However, neither liquor nor tobacco should be prohibited; instead, a sensible long-term campaign of public education should be entered into which would enable future generations to more nearly free themselves from these scourges of public addictions.

For, if man is to survive on this planet and, as he so survives becomes individually and collectively concerned with the future, then these various drug addictions must be relegated back into the dimension of normal usage—not as a collective group of agencies used in common escape mechanisms to relieve the individual from his pressurized civilization.

The problem of eliminating these various human frailties such as drug addiction, gambling and various vices does not lie within the dimension of forced elimination or suppression; all the laws and law enforcement agencies in the world have proven quite inadequate and useless to cope with these various human derelictions. Likewise, to continue on such a path of suppression will be equally sterile of results.

The only correct and intelligent answer is in education. If the growing child could be made to realize the full impact that his various life transpositions had upon his future—that he was actually making this future and that he was morally responsible to himself and to the society in which he lives, then these great human problems would begin to disappear.

As of today, no growing child lives in such an atmosphere; present-day living and educational methods are strictly reactionary and do not contain all the necessary elements of personal, moral values. Nor do they contain basic psychological values which every child should have from the cradle, up through his growing years; not as a part of a credit system in some college course, but a day to day learning and usage of a psychology which would acquaint the child with the very nature of his being—the reason for all things and his position in this infinite scale.

When all these things were so compounded together with the inevitable personal results or consequences which everyone faces in his future, the child would grow up with a great sense of moral responsibility. He would know that there was either a wonderful future for himself or, upon the same wheel of karma, he would always reap the pain of incomprehensive action.

He would know that this action was as conclusive as the seasons, the rise and fall of the tides, the cyclic movements of the planets and the very stars. For indeed it is the very stuff from which he is made, and was so ordered by himself and only he can change it.

Thus the child would grow; his life not a reactionary fear-filled day by day life of grasping, selfish attitudes, but a comprehensive, long-range plan of life which would unfold day by day in the full richness of infinite supply; and in this abundance, he would not crave with false appetite nor would he try to relieve these appetites with substitutes.

He would know the true meaning of cause and effect, of good and evil, his religion would not be one of some age-old mystic cult; but instead, would become a scientific composition of elements and factors which are a part and function of this Infinite Creative Intelligence. Life would become an active, ever-expanding participation in this Creation, not ending in some drug-steeped hell-hole of iniquity.

Let us then give all possible aid to this common cause of freedom, mental and spiritual emancipation from the carnal lusts of a material world.

CHAPTER 21

Sermons in Stones

It must be thoroughly understood by everyone who wishes to attain a higher way of life and for an individual to emancipate into one of the long-dreamed-of and hoped for Heavenly places—the great spiritual worlds—that he must do so along one common pathway of knowledge and through the doorway of wisdom.

It is clearly indicated that no person could live in some higher spiritual world if he were unfamiliar with the mode and way of living in such a place. No person can live in an environment which is foreign to his nature and with which he is not compatible in his expressive way of life. Therefore, on these premises, any person who so wishes to acquire this immortality and freedom from the vicissitudes from his fleshly earth life must begin first to thoroughly acquaint himself with the true nature of the Infinite Creator whom most people call God.

Knowledge of this Infinite Creator is, contrary to general opinion, not found through the doorway of some church or temple but is found in the ordinary manners and forms of various living attitudes. The Infinite Creator is supremely wise in all manners and forms of expression and it was in this Creative Intelligence that the earth was so conceived and dedicated as a place in which man could begin to learn the elemental principles of this Creative Intelligence.

To begin your flight into Eternity then, you must by all means, become acquainted with the Infinite Creative Intelligence as it functions in all manners and forms of life about you in your daily world. It is enigmatic that by far, most people go from the cradle to the grave without knowing even the most rudimentary or elemental knowledge of this great Intelligent Creation which is taking place all around them every moment of their lives.

Let us take, for a moment, a specific example to better understand this Creative Intelligence. Some years ago, a group of scientists who were probing to find some answer to the riddle of creation performed the following experiment: they took a large wooden tub or box and placed into it, a certain quantity of thoroughly dried earth which was carefully weighed to the last gram and the amount recorded; then in this earth they planted a tree, a small sapling about two feet tall and, after carefully watering and caring for the tree for a number of years, they removed the tree including the roots from the earth, carefully brushing away every speck of earth. They again weighed this earth in the tub and found that the difference in weight from the time the tree was planted was only two ounces. After drying and weighing the tree, it was found to weigh more than twelve hundred pounds— more than half a ton of woody substance called cellulose. Here was a great mystery. What was the Creative Intelligence this tree expressed? How did this tree take the substances of minerals and vitamins from the earth and combine them with energy from the sun, together with certain molecules of gas from the air and make from these various substances a tremendous amount of heavy wood fiber? No doubt the scientists are still pondering the answer.

And while you, too, are pondering this answer, let us turn our point of introspection to your own body, for here again is one of the innumerable miracles which are constantly taking place all about you and which you have taken more or less for granted. If you live to be threescore and ten, or seventy years, you will have made during that time ten complete bodies. The remanufacture or replacement of your body includes not only the fleshly portions and the blood-stream, but also includes all of the bones in the skeleton structure of your frame—the skull, leg bones, arms—everything about you has been replaced ten times. This you have done without even your conscious knowledge of having done so. This automatic function was taking place at the rate of about one million, five hundred thousand cells per minute which were dying and being replaced in this physical anatomy in which you are presently living.

Now, the solution to this great mystery is quite easily found, if we can lift the horizon of our mental introspection beyond the confines of our third dimensional world, and looking over the fence of materialism, so to speak, we shall see that you, just as in the case of the tree which grew in the tub, or with any other particular plant or animal life which grows upon the face of the earth, that each and every one of these objects have what is called a psychic anatomy; and it is in this psychic anatomy that we find the true answer to this great enigma. The psychic anatomy is an amalgamated collection of different kinds of energy which are compounded therein in vortexes and these little energies so revolving as wave forms, in a gyrating, centrifugal motion within these vortexes, are constantly repeating the idiom of their information or intelligence until they, too, are either replaced or that they will, as a natural consequence, pass into oblivion.

The tree spent many thousands of years in the development of its own particular, specific form of evolution. This was done through various environmental pressures under which it grew from time to time in different earth lives. For the psychic body or anatomy of the tree repropagated itself as a form of exterior consciousness into this third dimensional world as one of the functions of the Supreme Creative Intelligence which was constantly stemming into it from a higher or fifth dimensional world.

The same process is quite true with you in your present state of evolution or development; the various organs and structures of your physical anatomy were developed by you, in combination with various associations and environmental pressures from almost time immemorial or the beginning of your evolution, when you began to sustain a direct continuity of ego-consciousness as a definite polarity with this psychic anatomy in conjunction with the higher and more Infinite Creative Source.

It can now be clearly seen that the function of the third dimensional world is not, in any sense, the complete function of any species of plant or animal life; no more so than is true in these various expressive continuities in which various plant and animal species so live and survive upon the planet earth. For therein, too, is great intelligence in this creative expression, and if we study the biology of various different plant and animal life upon the face of this planet, we will find that there is a great amount of intelligence being constantly expressed; not only individually, as it concerns a species of plant or animal, but in the way in which certain balances are maintained throughout this terrestrial dimension.

The carnivorous animals prey and feed upon the herbivorous so that a balance is maintained. This balance is likened somewhat to the law or principle of supply and demand; and wherever we go upon this earth, we shall see this great system of balances constantly in effect which controls any abnormal tendencies; for growth in any particular species which would enable it to overrun the earth, would produce a great and devastating effect.

Therefore, in the future as you develop along this pathway of life, the common pathway of knowledge and understanding will lead you to and through the doorway of wisdom into some higher spiritual world. You will gradually begin to learn the constituents of intelligence as they are expressed in energy wave forms and, as we have often presented the obvious fact, which is quite well known scientifically at this day and age: there is no such thing as a solid substance and all solid substances should be resolved into tiny energy constituents called atoms, which are miniature solar systems. These atoms are being controlled directly by certain psychic bodies which the atoms possess, as do all other substances found on the surface of the earth.

This psychic body of the atom is quite similar in many respects to the psychic bodies found in all other plant and animal life—that is, aside from its own particular size. It maintains the same centrifugal or vortexal fashion of which all other particular forms of expressive energy motion are so currently formed in this fourth or higher dimensional form; and here again, in the atom, is a direct transference of intelligence—which is the true nature of the atom—from this psychic vortex, into the third dimensional world. It makes little difference whether we analyze the atom or whether we analyze a sun, a planetary system, a galaxy or a large number of galaxies, the pattern here is quite similar and analogous in all cases. We will find the same great conflux of interdimensional vortexes of energy which contain the vast and incalculable number of energy wave forms, all of which are so oriented with themselves to the basis of frequency and polarities as to form a very intelligent and re-creative pattern of expression into the lower third dimensional worlds.

Therefore, in the future days to come, it would be

well to look about you in your various daily forms of expressions and motions of your life to see the cause and reason for all things behind these seemingly insoluble enigmas as they have so confounded you up until the present time. You, like countless millions of others, have noted the same enigmatical differences which would and could remain insoluble until the end of time, unless such patterns of analysis are followed which would lead you into fourth dimensional translations of life about you. Look into the form and substance of your daily life about you and see—not the surface as it so manifests itself directly as a reactionary form and substance but—a much deeper and heretofore hidden meaning which is the fourth or higher dimensional aspect of this reactionary form and motion which is going on about you. See the psychic anatomies of all plant and animal species; that everything possesses these psychic bodies—even the stones and the planet earth itself are only an outside configuration of the same psychic embodiments which we have described to you.

When you have begun to master this concept, then indeed your life will begin to change and you will find your feet firmly planted upon that pathway of knowledge and in your future incarnations, whether they concern terrestrial lives or lives between earth lives in higher dimensions, you will find a direct proportion of intelligence coming your way and which will be impounded in your psychic anatomy; and thus your new spiritual body will begin to grow and develop— a body which will enable you to live in these higher spiritual worlds.

CHAPTER 22

Fuels or Fools?

There can be no doubt in the mind of any person but that we have entered well into a new scientific age; for everywhere about us are the many manifestations of this technocracy. Cities and the highways which link these cities contain vast evidence of this new age of science and the very skies are now used as highroads for various devices of communications brought about by this science. Yes, even the small children play about in space suits and helmets, riding rockets through imaginary skies to distant planets.

Several of these much talked about scientific achievements or projects are, however, still dreams which have yet to be fulfilled. Heading the list of these dreams is atomic power; for despite various developments in nuclear weapons, power plants and atomically powered submarines, man is still far from his goal in achieving an abundance of cheap atomic power. For the present and future generations, comes the idea of the vast and staggering proportions of this need and which can be gathered from some currently available statistics.

During the past sixty years, utility companies in the United States have been forced to double their kilowatt power output once every eight years. The chief source of electric and various other thermal power sources come from fossil fuels, coal or petroleum products and, according to the present rise in population, the sources of fossil fuels will be exhausted in less than 100 years, should these population increases continue at their current rate. This has caused a vastly accelerated search for some available source of cheap power which can fully and adequately meet the demands of the rising population.

It must also be remembered that in the case of fossil fuel consumption there is also a great concern over the problem of air pollution from various chemical deposits blown into the atmosphere by the use of fossil fuel. This has practically mandated strict curtailment of the use of this type of fuel in certain heavily populated areas which are at the present time wrestling with this air pollution-smog problem. This condition mandates that future expansion of power facilities will have to take place in the direction which can produce cheap electrical power without burning the fossil fuel to acquire it.

At first, to the layman, atomic power seems a very feasible solution for a cheap and abundant source of electrical power, produced from various nuclear reactors or furnaces; however, the problems here, too, are very great and, for the present, represent certain insurmountable objections. First, we must understand how atomic power can be produced. At the present time, there are two known ways of producing atomic power. These are nuclear fission and nuclear fusion and in principle, they are directly opposite to each other.

Nuclear fission means that power is released when a certain unstable isotope atom, such as U-235, is torn or blown apart, releasing a certain quanta of energy in the form of heat. Such nuclear fission produces temperatures of 100 million degrees centigrade.

The other type of nuclear reaction is nuclear

fusion, which means that two atoms such as the unstable atom isotope called heavy water, fuses with another similar atom. The two atoms literally implode together. This fusion process has been dramatically demonstrated in the explosion of the hydrogen bomb, with temperatures running into at least 500 million degrees centigrade. This type of nuclear reaction has been going on in the sun and various stars for billions of years, or at least the present-day scientist believes this is what is taking place.

The implosion of hydrogen atoms, one into the other, creates a new atom called helium. The outside or surface of this process has been carefully observed and watched by the physicist using our nearby star-sun as the basic point of his inspection. In various texts of Unarius, a more accurate picture of this nuclear process is described; the various atoms being formed under tremendous electromagnetic stresses and processes from the interior of a great fourth dimensional vortex. The truth of these facts has already been partially verified by the existing knowledge that our present-day scientist has at his disposal; and from the nuclear process he has observed occurring in the chromosphere of the sun, he has succeeded in creating a hydrogen bomb. However, to make a hydrogen bomb explode, he must trigger it by using an atom bomb, just as the powder in a rifle cartridge burns when it is triggered by a small explosion caused by the firing pin when it strikes a small quantity of mercury fulminate imbedded on the inside of the cap.

Now, the problems with atomic power are specifically this: in the case of nuclear fission, there is always a precipitation of radioactive wastes. Some of these are in the form of solids, others are gaseous. The future power needs of the world, a hundred years from now, are estimated to be equivalent to all the power which could be generated by 20,000 million atom bombs per year, of the highest strength yet produced. The use of that much atomic fission would render the earth completely radioactive in a few months time and all forms of life would vanish because of the vast amounts of radioactive waste produced by this tremendous atomic fission.

Even our present needs, if they were fully met by such fissionable atomic power, would soon render the earth unfit for human habitation. Moreover, the question of producing such power is very tricky. It is simply an accumulation of a certain amount of U-235, which is placed in a furnace surrounded by liquid; then this material is triggered into a nuclear reaction. This reaction is controlled by inserting or withdrawing bars of cadmium. However, U-235 is notoriously unstable. It may either be triggered or else it may suddenly go wild and blow a fifty foot crater where the power plant once stood. Even if things go well, the radioactive ash must be taken care of; this is also very tricky business.

At the present time, this disposal problem is quite acute even with a comparatively small amount of experimentation and usage which is engaged in, in present-day experimental needs. Some of this waste is placed in weighted cans and hauled out to sea by ships and dumped. However, this waste remains radioactive for over sixty years. During that time, the cans can rust away or be exploded by the generation of gas inside the can.

The problem of producing power from nuclear fusion seems much more practical inasmuch as such fusion leaves no radioactive waste or, at least, controlled amounts of strontium 90. The useful helium gas is the end product. The problem of creating such power is, however, practically insurmountable, simply because the production of such power must take place in a furnace in a sustained or continuous condition and burned at a temperature in excess of one hundred million degrees.

A similar chemical condition occurs when we combine ordinary hydrogen with oxygen and heat these two combined gases to a temperature of several thousand degrees. Under these conditions, hydrogen and oxygen will burn or chemically unite, producing the byproduct of common water, H^2-O. However, this chemical process is just as tricky as it is in the case of a sustained hydrogen burning process.

One more point in favor of obtaining power from nuclear fusion or hydrogen is the source of supply. In the case of fissionable materials—uranium, radium and thorium—this supply is very limited and would be exhausted within the next few years if it were used to meet even existing power demands. The amount of available hydrogen is practically unlimited. Heavy water, or hydrogen too, can feasibly be extracted from ocean water.

It is estimated that the available amount of heavy water which could be extracted from the ocean would meet all power needs upon the earth for the next ten thousand billion years or the present estimated age of the universe. There are, however, other problems confronting the physicist in the production of cheap power by hydrogen fusion. A practical furnace would have to be built from materials which could withstand the extreme temperatures of this sustained condition of over 100 million degrees.

This is far beyond the melting point of any known elements and any furnace built from existing materials would vanish in a puff of smoke long before it was hot enough to sustain hydrogen fusion, for the walls of the furnace must be at least 100 million degrees, otherwise the hydrogen would be cooled and fusion could not occur.

One of the possible solutions which our present-day scientists hope will be the answer to this problem is that project known as the "magnetic bottle". In other words, he hopes to create a hydrogen furnace by lining it with a layer of strong magnetic energy. However, as of this time, he has not succeeded in creating a sufficiently dense magnetic field which would effectively prevent the hydrogen atoms from escaping between the magnetic lines of force. As one scientist put it, "It is like trying to hold a gob of warm jelly in a vessel made of rubber bands."

Now, it is quite evident that the dream of cheap atomic power is far from becoming a reality and it will take at least several years more before the scientist can definitely state "yes" or "no" to this problem; and as of this time he is still confronted with years of research, building and re-building, trial and error, before he is even close to the solution of cheap atomic power. It is wonderful to say that there are several thousand million horsepower in a glassful of heavy water but science is still far from realizing this potential.

Meanwhile the scientists are probing into other ways and means of obtaining this cheap power. The most popular way would be to obtain energy from an already existing hydrogen furnace—the sun. However, vast as this sun power is, it would still take a tremendous outlay of money to relieve even one small fraction of our present needs; using present-day solar cells, we would have to cover the states of Utah, Arizona, New Mexico and Colorado completely with these solar cells and at present prices, this would cost in excess of two hundred thousand billion dollars; in effect, more money than that presently possessed by this country in Fort Knox.

Solar furnaces which concentrate the sun's energies are also not feasible for the same basic reason of cost. It is much more expensive to produce a kilowatt of energy from a solar furnace than it is from a group of solar cells.

In summing up this entire discussion, we can say

liberally that science has provided many new and wonderful things for us to use in the everyday world; but the fancied Utopian dreams of an "atomic age" still vanish in the lack of present-day knowledge of how to make these dreams come true.

CHAPTER 23

The Cosmic Centrifuge

In the foregoing article we entered into a frank discussion of certain relative problems which confronted the nuclear physicist at this present time in his attempt to duplicate solar energy and to create for the world an abundance of power. The various statistics were drawn from up-to-the-minute scientific findings and summaries of these findings. The author does not vouch for their accuracy; instead, he would like to point out these various findings of today are just as inaccurate as the findings of yesterday which have been replaced by the present findings.

For instance, but a few years ago the mean temperature of the sun was believed to be 35 million degrees. Today scientists think it may be three or four hundred million degrees. The truth is, they do not know, simply because the temperature of the sun cannot be measured, for it has no temperature; as a matter of fact, heat itself is a complete illusion just as are all of the various other elements involved in present-day scientific concepts.

In previous texts presented by the author, numerous references were made to an obvious and conclusive fact: that all existing third dimensional elements including heat and light, could be properly understood only when they were reduced to their original source as pure energy; and that atoms, heat, light and sound are only secondary regenerations of these various interdimensional energies.

To measure heat—as is commonly supposed to exist by science—means that we must place a thermocouple into this so-called hydrogen source. This thermocouple consists of a metal rod which is actually composed of two strips of different kinds of metal welded together and attached to this rod; on one end is a copper wire which conducts electricity to a meter which has a dial marked off in numbers and a moving pointer. When the metal rod is placed in the heat source, the atoms in the two different kinds of metal begin to vibrate more rapidly. This causes a certain plus-minus condition in electromagnetic fields which is expressed as a quantum of electrical energy, which travels up the wire into the meter causing the pointer to move forward according to how much energy is being conducted by the metal rod.

It is obvious that the scientist does not possess a thermo-couple which would reach across 93 million miles of space whereby he could more accurately measure this so-called heat. Even if he were able to do so, the metal rod would be instantly disintegrated because it could not compensate for the extreme energy conduction which it would have to undergo if it were plunged into the chromosphere of the sun. This means then that the scientist has had to calculate according to certain reactive conditions which he has set up on the surface of the earth. This is something like trying to measure heat from a candle flame burning in a nearby state. It has not occurred to the scientist, despite his knowledge of electrical energies, that heat is a certain quantum of energy, produced by first creating some kind of hysteresis into a group of atomic constituents.

This hysteresis re-creates certain secondary harmonics which, in radiating from the reactive mass of atoms, must come in contact with another mass of

142

atoms and again create the secondary set of harmonic regenerations. This second set of regenerations is thought by the scientist to be heat.

Take an ordinary thermometer for instance: it is a glass tube container and a small drop of mercury. Mercury is a metal which is liquid at ordinary temperatures. The inside of the glass tube is a complete vacuum. Now, certain wave forms of electrical energy pass through the electromagnetic fields of the various atoms which comprise the air surrounding the outside surface of the glass tube. This creates a secondary group of energy wave forms. These, in turn, strike and radiate into the electromagnetic fields of atoms comprising the glass walls of the tube; finally, into the mercury itself.

When these secondary wave forms strike the electromagnetic fields of the atoms of mercury, they become excited and expand. They puff up, as it were, in their attempt to absorb this extra energy. This energy is not heat because the mercury does not become hot. However, it does rise in the tube because of the expansion. Like water, mercury will vaporize if it absorbs too much energy. In all cases, that which the scientist believes to be heat is only a certain reactive condition involving the expansion of various atoms because they absorb a certain quantum of energy and the rate of absorption is called by the scientist, heat. He has not measured the cause of this expansion; he has only compared its effect in his relationship to other types of similar effects which are going on around him. Therefore, heat is actually nonexistent as is light and various other factors connected with the currently existing theories of science. While there are very apparent contradictions everywhere about us, in more immediate relative terms as they concern everyone, let us point out other and greater contradictions which exist in the present-day nuclear physics.

Just as we have previously discussed, the scientist

is trying to build a nuclear furnace which he can use to create power by nuclear fusion. He knows that there is a huge ball of energy hanging in the sky which he calls the sun, which is already producing vast amounts of energy, and has been for many billions of years; and so far as he knows, it will continue to do so for many more billions of years.

It seems very apparent at this moment that this great solar nuclear fusion furnace is so functioning in complete violation of his presently known laws of nuclear physics; for this sun is so functioning—according to science—in a complete vacuum which (also according to the scientist), must have a mean temperature of minus 473 degrees, or absolute zero. How then does the scientist compensate for this obvious contradiction?

In his fusion furnace, which he hopes to build, he must maintain a temperature of 100 million degrees plus, in the area with the immediate atomically fusing hydrogen. He knows if the walls of his furnace are cooler than this temperature, fusion stops. How then does the sun maintain its constant steady state of fusion in a temperature of absolute zero?

Also while we are asking questions, what originally gave the sun its trigger-action of 100 million or more degrees; and what unknown force keeps this triggering action going on? Of course the scientist cannot answer these questions; but far worse than this display of ignorance are his continued efforts to synthetically create a nuclear science based upon this same ignorance. Amazingly enough, the scientist has already partially created a nuclear fusion furnace in an entirely different and unsuspected area of his nuclear science, specifically; the cyclotron which was created by the scientists in their attempt to split the atom.

A cyclotron is simply a huge circle of very powerful horseshoe magnets. By using a stream of electrical energy, these magnets begin to kick this energy around within the circumference of this circle between their various respective poles. This is done by creating oscillating positive and negative conditions in respect to the passing electrical energies. This action accelerates the electrons which comprise this energy, to a point where they assume incredible speed and are shot into certain kinds of atoms, similar in theory to rifle bullets, hoping that by chance one of these bullets will strike the core of another atom and split it. What the scientist hopes to achieve by this is still rather vague, even to the scientist. He has yet to achieve any kind of a direct photographic or other reactive knowledge of what actually happens when an atom is split.

This whole procedure is very analogous to a man who takes his automobile apart to see what makes it run, when he could sit down in his easy chair and read a book all about automobiles; so it is with the scientist, as the evidence of cosmic hysteresis is like an open book everywhere about him and the relationship of the atom to this cosmic hysteresis is also quite evidential. There is no need to take his atomic atom apart; no more than the small boy who takes his watch apart to see what makes it tick.

Getting back to the cyclotron—the scientist has in effect partially created a fusion furnace and, from the basic knowledge which we have given in various Unarius texts, he could complete the construction of this cyclotron into such a fusion furnace. Many times we have presented the picture (in other Unarius writings), of cosmic hysteresis and how our third dimensional atomic and electronic worlds were created.

Vortexes of fourth dimensional energy concentrate in their center a tremendously compressed nuclei of this energy which would be an atom, or a sun according to the size and complexity of the vortex which so created it. If the scientist would take his cyclotron and enclose it in a chamber, then completely evacuate from this chamber all atoms of oxygen and other gases involved, then replace this vacuum with the hydrogen isotope, heavy water—now by starting to kick these atoms around like a centrifuge inside the chamber of the cyclotron, he could in effect create a synthetic vortex, very much like that which first created and sustained the sun. By using certain plus and minus charges in an oscillating ionization process, these various hydrogen atoms would be continuously impelled toward the center of the vortex where they would accumulate and be compressed until they formed a nucleus of pure fusion energy, very similar to the sun.

Moreover, this compression could be controlled; any temperature desired could be constituted and maintained in the nucleus by controlling the plus and minus ionization process which impelled atomic particles toward this nucleus. The energy which was so generated could be absorbed by a glorified thermocouple and conducted, as electrical energy, from the nucleus to the outside of the chamber by means of an ordinary conducting cable. In effect then, the scientist would have created a synthetic vortex, very similar to any and all vortexes which are sustaining our third dimensional world. However, the type of fusion furnace we have described is only one way to achieve this same end. The earth itself could be made into such a centrifuge.

In two past civilizations, now unknown to science, the earth was made into a cosmic centrifuge. This was done in the following manner: on certain predetermined points around the circumference of the earth, there were erected certain magnetic structures. As the earth turned on its axis, the polarities of these various magnetic structures were changed or oscillated. This condition cut or intercepted various lines of electromagnetic force surrounding the earth. This action, in turn, induced tremendous energy into certain kinds of "pickup" coils functioning in conjunction with the magnetic structures.

This process is amazingly similar to the electro-magnetic generator which Henry Ford built into every Model T car; and strange indeed that here again, science has the answer to its greatest problems in the most common and simplest devices which surround him on every side. The Model T Ford generator functioned this way: a ring of these magnets was placed around the periphery of the flywheel. A copper ribbon was then wound around a series of iron pole pieces, fastened to the periphery of another disc, the same diameter as the flywheel. This disc was then closely placed to the flywheel on the same axial plane.

When the flywheel rotated, the magnets generated a certain cut and re-cut condition of magnetic lines intercepted by the pole pieces or, as induced magnetic currents. These in turn were picked up or conducted by the copper ribbon coil wound around this pole piece and finally, in a series arrangement, terminated to one common point. The fly-wheel, rotating one hundred or a thousand times a minute, then produced sufficient alternating current to energize the electrical spark system and also to light the head and tail lights of the car. The amount of power of course was always determined by the flywheel revolutions.

The scientist of the future therefore could convert the earth to the same type of an electromagnetic generator. It is synonymous to any type of aircraft or space vehicle which he will use in this future. The flying saucer functions according to this same principle; first getting its initial power from such an electromagnetic generator as we have so described and it, in turn, using its power to create strong magnetic force fields which would impel the ship in any direction.

Back in the Atlantean civilization, as well as in the Lemurian civilization which was actually the father-mother of Atlantis, these great cosmic electromagnetic generators functioned perfectly without being attended or being watched over for thousands of years. They

147

supplied an abundance of cost-free power to the great cities of these civilizations.

Twelve thousand years B.C., the Atlantean civilization perished and was totally destroyed when a certain race of people succeeded in stealing certain of the electromagnetically powered spaceships; and in their ignorance, misused them in a concentrated attack which generated an oscillating condition with these great generators. The resulting explosion was a cataclysmic catastrophe which actually shifted the axis of the earth, created holes in the ocean floor, raised up great mountain ranges and created many other geographical changes which are still seen in this present day. This history contains an indirect warning to the scientist of tomorrow. When and should he ever arrive at the point in his science whereby he has created this cosmic generator, he will also have to have a complete and unified system of living for the peoples of the earth.

The vast potentials and possibilities of such unlimited cosmic power could be very tempting to certain people who would take it to gain control of the earth, and the history of Atlantis could be repeated. Therefore, take heed; along with scientific achievement there must also be social achievement; advancement in scientific technocracy must always be equalized by similar advances in the social atmosphere and the environment in which such technocracy exists.

While it is evident that such various scientific advances were created for the common usage of mankind and to better his general environment, these same scientific advances could also be, inversely, the means of his destruction if he does not properly use and safeguard them against the ever-present possibility of misuse by certain individuals or groups who may be tempted with false lusts and purposes.

CHAPTER 24

Judge Not

It has been observed in this humble cliché, that every dog has his day and while this observation may seemingly have involved members of the canine world, there is a much deeper and more philosophical content which could be applied in various cyclic movements involving mankind, individually or collectively. Whether they concerned the rise and fall of civilizations, or more individualistic expressions such as kings, emperors, ruling deities, religions, hierarchies and politicos, they too, also lived in their day and vanished in time. While such various expressions and re-expressions always idiomatically assumed the environmental form of the race which so produced it or into such singular expressionists so connected, the principles behind such resurgent cyclic movements were and are basically the same and are as true today as they were when they happened many thousands of years ago.

To understand then these basic principles which engender cyclic movement either individually or as they are resumed in the collective masses of some civilization, we will always find the underlying motions of such cyclic movements, whether progressive or retrogressive, as comprising delicately balanced equilibriums between two widely divergent polarities of life—good and evil. In a progressive evolutionary movement as it concerns the development of a race of people, a civilization or any singular person, any progressive balances which can be called good or constructive must be maintained in order to offset the corrosive action of the negative or evil polarity.

While in ordinary evaluations, such opposites as good and evil are highly contradictory to each other in either form or appearance, yet in a more abstract evaluation, one is as necessary as the other. Briefly then, such polarities refer to such expressive movements of various forms and their motional impedances as traveling in two different directions; and such motional impedances which are set up in either of these motions always make their appearance upon the surface of life, either as a constructive element or a destructive one. While, on the surface, these two appearances may present an enigma, it must be remembered (as was stated), that one is just as necessary as the other and so far as surface appearances are concerned, any such constructive values which you now may possess could be called negative by comparison in the appearances of more highly developed constructive appearances.

In other words, good and evil are only a system of comparisons as they relate to any emotional appearances of life; and it is well to consider many known and sometimes unknown factors which may be involved before jumping to hasty conclusions. Therefore, in such personal evaluations as they concern the planet earth, the many races of people which have come and gone, their method of interpreting life on earth has been maintained on certain basic levels and these levels of interpretation are just the same today as they were thousands of years ago.

By comparison, in various social levels as they appear at the present time, we could say that the so-called intellect who graduates from a great university is little different than the dark-skinned aborigine in the far-off jungle. This evaluation may sound startling but will appear as fact when a more complete analysis is made into the various subconscious reflex actions which motivate both men; and in the college graduate we find the same set of subconscious reflexes as are found in the savage.

Therefore, the great difference with the so-called intellectual, lies purely within the realm of surface developments. He possesses a certain amount of knowledge which was incurred in his educational process. However, he is in no wise possessed of a more purely constructive mind than is the black man and the basic reference level for any thinking process is subconscious comparisons. The constructive aptitude of either man is in no wise different unless we take our analysis and probe far deeper into the lives of either individual. Here we will find the true differences.

The college graduate may be one of the more advanced intellects, and, in his evolutionary pathway through thousands of past lifetimes, he will have gained sufficient knowledge and affiliations with higher spiritual worlds as well as a more direct aptitude to function with the higher superconscious self which will make him different than the jungle savage. In fact, it will make him different from his fellow graduates, as well as most of the population of the world.

And here again we find a more striking difference between such polarities as can be considered good or evil; for in any case where an individual reaches the attainment or function with the Higher Self, he can be considered, therefore, one of these higher, more positive polarities of which we have spoken. Conversely, any other individual not so possessing this working contact with the Higher Self is an evil or destructive entity and when such a person individually or collectively meets one of these Higher Creative Entities there is an immediate, sometimes explosive, reaction which takes place.

In other words, the negative entity feels a deflation of

ego; he does not understand either the working of the higher mind or its higher constructivism. He is confronted by the obvious fact that his values of life are inferior by comparison. He then becomes a classical rhetorician. He will seek in one form or another to declaim the higher expression and the expressionist. If he is supported en masse by a group who is also rhetorical, the effect might well be a quick and drastic elimination of the higher expressionist. This has been very dramatically expressed in a number of historical configurations. The number of constructionists who function from the higher level have always been few and far between in comparison with the masses of humanity who so express themselves likewise.

To quote a few specific examples, let us first turn to Jesus of Nazareth and how his constructive mission on earth was drastically climaxed in murder brought about by the rabbinical rhetoricians of the temple. Again the spotlight of attention goes back much further into history—more than a thousand years before Jesus. An Egyptian Pharaoh named Akhenaton, was purged from the face of the earth through the poison cup by the hierarchy of priests, the old order of rhetoricians, who returned Egypt to its old black magic.

Buddha died unknown except in his own province, for his views about obtaining junction with the Higher Self, or Nirvana, were too advanced for the rhetoricians of his time. Not until 250 years later did King Asoka bring forth the teachings of Buddha. (And was not King Asoka, Buddha reincarnate?) Yet this king had hardly been laid to rest upon his death before rhetoricians had already begun their deadly work. Soon the simple teachings of Nirvana began to be compounded with an ever increasing number of devious ways of attainment and paths to follow. Today Buddha lives in the Temples of India with more than thirty million other gods, all produced by the rhetorical mind.

Socrates, too, found death through the poisoned cup forced upon him (or banishment) by the rhetoricians of his time. Julius Caesar, a constructionist, found death at the hands of his son by a cleverly engineered plot conceived by the master rhetorician, Cassius, who was jealous of Caesar and his accomplishments and Brutus, made a malcontent by believing his mother was Caesar's concubine, performed the historical mission of destruction.

Found in every rhetorical mind is the desire to destroy or tear down that which is not understood; and there are countless thousands of recorded and unrecorded examples of rhetorical destruction throughout the Middle Ages. Through the hierarchy of a great church which functioned either independently or through the courts of inquisition thousands of persons were, plundered and murdered. Millions were burned at the stake, torn on the rack or hung on the gallows by command of the rhetorical minds whose power came from those who wore the robes; and in their self-deification, erected great preponderant systems of rhetorical elements.

Thus as it has always been through countless years of time, epochs and ages, the rise and fall of civilizations, all have had their constructionists and, while all of these constructionists have made vital contributions to the posterity of mankind, yet inevitably have they been destroyed by those who benefited the most. And unable to understand this beneficent action, they retaliated and reacted in the typical rhetorical way.

To those who read these or any pages so brought forth by this author, let them take heed and warning. While consciously to yourselves you may be drawn to the higher expressions of life, you may acknowledge this higher way; you may even claim to be expressionists of this higher way. Such as you are, by your fruits ye shall be known and let not this fruit contain the bitter gall of the rhetorical mind, even though your inclinations, your aspirations and idealisms are of the highest. There is still much to learn and understand; and failure to learn or understand will create within you a possible negative attunement and through this attunement, the old, subconscious, lower, rhetorical self will strike. You may feel these destructive blows either as mild criticisms or comparisons with other things which you understand better; or you may strike the heaviest of all reactionary blows—complete condemnation.

In any case however, dear soul, whether this blow be light or heavy, it is one which you have struck against yourself. You, not I, shall feel its impact. You will feel it in the years to come; for as these blows strike within your mind, they will destroy your temple and one which you have to painstakingly and, with tears and sweat, rebuild in future lives.

No man's opinion can change the face of Truth, for Truth remains inviolate, a complete function of the Infinite Mind. Each man, in daily thought and action, interprets some infinitesimally small portion of Truth into his daily life and he can, conversely, by denying any such expressions of Infinite action or wisdom, close himself off from this ever-sustaining Life Force.

If you do not understand, do not condemn that which you do not understand but condemn only your own ignorance. The Infinite is just that—Infinite—and in no man's mind or hands lies the power to take from or add to this Infinite.

CHAPTER 25

Mass — The Illusion

It has often (and very truly) been said, that of all the enigmas in the universe of human understanding, man himself is the greatest. This is so, for despite the fact that of the many thousands of years in which man has inhabited the planet earth and in these thousands of years, he has spent tremendous time and effort in trying to understand himself; as of today, he is still confronted with this inescapable paradox. This seems a bit ridiculous, for in viewing the many advanced factors and concepts which are at the disposal of everyone, yet life still goes on basically much the same as it always has.

Principles of life in personal relationships are functioning just as inviolately as they always have. Perhaps the greatest part of this great enigma could be found in such kindred fields as human endeavor, which are commonly referred to as the healing professions, such as materia medica and such adjacent divisions of psychology, etcetera. For despite great hospitals, the advanced techniques in medicine, surgery and psychology, the modern doctor reluctantly admits he knows only about 25 percent of what goes on in the human body. Whether it is medicine or a more general classification of sciences, the enigma remains just as great; great, because man is constantly surrounded, at all times, with all of the answers which would solve this enigma. As a matter of fact, science holds within its hands all of the keys to the wisdom of the Infinite, yet it does not apparently know either how to use or to understand them correctly.

Some years ago, a man named Einstein gave an advanced theory that mass was an illusion and that everything was, after all, energy. This was later proven in our nuclear science. The implications and ramifications of this concept are infinitely broad but are reducible to some very easily understood factors.

First, as all things are energy, to learn the secrets of life will therefore mean that we, as individuals, who would like to learn these secrets, must begin to understand energy. This is quite true, not only with the individual truth seeker, but also with the future materia medica and psychologists; for, while in the present tense this materia medica and attendant therapeutic practices literally hold the power of life and death over hundreds of millions of people, yet, without exception, no practitioner understands or applies such an understanding of these electronic principles in his daily practice.

No exceptions are made for X-rays, square sine wave generators, encephalographs, heat lamps and such. These are all comparatively crude; their function is only partly understood, even less in most cases by the operator.

A large number of so-called incurable diseases will therefore remain to plague mankind until that future day when the doctor becomes a true scientist and deals with each patient as a composite amalgamation of electronic forms and their attendant functions; for every human being is this, and nothing more. His body is composed of a large group of atoms, each one a tiny solar system of energy, supported in its power and function by a vortex of energy which functions in an adjacent dimension (the psychic anatomy).

To better understand these principles of life, we will

156

divide energy into two classifications; the "static" or atomic form, composed of various kinds of electrons in a solar system and the "dynamic" or moving forms of energy. These can be reclassified as light or electricity which travels at 186,000 miles per second, to the slower forms of energy like sound.

In all cases however, static or dynamic, the principle of integration of consciousness is contained in the frequency rate, or the number of times which any energy wave form or atom vibrates in a positive to negative to positive fashion. In the fourth or adjacent dimensions, all such polarity expressions are carried in a cyclic form. This means that they contain within themselves, their own time factor which, as the cyclic form, retunes itself, so to speak, like links in a chain, with all other cyclic forms in the Infinite macrocosm and microcosm.

So far as our material or third dimensional wave forms are concerned, time is separate and assumes itself in the form of polarities, or a starting place and finishing place, called positive or negative. In any case, such starting and finishing places, as positive and negative, are only relative and are of concern only in our various interpolations of these energy constituents in our daily life.

In other words then, whether or not we are describing movements of any form of energy in any dimension, we must remember that the same principles hold true and are inviolate with every human being. The various processes of life connected with the five senses, are merely ways in which man individually intercepts and recombines various wave forms which come to him from the outside or exterior surface of his life, into the complex matrix of wave forms in the subconscious. On the basis of frequency relationship, these various wave forms are either immediately attuned to these various existing wave forms where they are reflected or regenerated into the conscious mind, or else they remain a disembodied form of consciousness in sort of a twilight zone.

This is more easily understood in this comparison: A person can see any familiar object; the process of oscillation from the subconscious into the conscious, which takes about one tenth of a second, is sort of a reshuffling process as the familiar or semi-familiar object is compared or scanned, as it were, through frequency attunement with other previously existing wave forms. If this person sees an unfamiliar object he at first does not believe what he sees; the wave forms of this unfamiliar object find no harmonic attunement in the subconscious and will remain suspended in the twilight zone until the person begins to rationalize. This means the person who has seen this unfamiliar object now sets up certain harmonic wave-trains which are, to some small or large degree, compatible on the basis of frequency with this unfamiliar object as it oscillates in the twilight zone.

This process of regenerating and recombining the harmonic elements of comparison may take only several minutes, or it may take years, or even a lifetime, depending primarily, of course, upon such factors as the number of existing wave forms already in the subconscious which can be harmonically attuned and recombined with the unknown elements in the twilight zone.

Herein enters another important principle of understanding. The conscious mind is not the brain. The brain is composed of about 50 billion cells which can be likened to small transistors or frequency integrators. When a wave form comes from the subconscious to the conscious, it must pass through various portions of the brain which contain cells particularly suited for this transference; the determinant here is frequency. Thus various anterior and posterior lobes or portions of the brain contain cells more suited to certain various reflexes. Here, in turn, the wave forms are reshuffled into another portion of the psychic anatomy which can be considered the true brain. Here is another grouping of vortexes which are harmonically attuned to another and even higher portion of this psychic anatomy—the Superconscious Self—or the facsimile of the Infinite. This conscious or brain portion of the psychic anatomy functions as follows: it has the power to determine or recombine various values on the basis of frequency, from past experiences from a large number of lifetimes through which the individual has passed.

In a sense, this is extending the power of consciousness far beyond the dimension of the present life which is more purely contained in the subconscious portion of the psychic anatomy. This is done, however, without the usual and more pronounced reflex action which always takes place in the subconscious function. This higher consciousness can therefore be considered to be not only the more true seat of reason but also expresses various other attributes, one of which is called intuition. In fact, all paranormal functions or activities of this mental or conscious part of the psychic anatomy come from this source.

There is one more important implication connected with this part of the psychic anatomy and that is its more direct function with the Superconscious. It is from this highest portion of the psychic anatomy that the individual derives such various elements of life which can be called creative or inspirational; or that they may even be, in this creative sense, a completely independent materialization of form into the surface life and not necessarily connected through frequency with any or all past life dispensations and experiences.

When this integration of consciousness is fully understood—how it functions as a complex integration of wave forms of energy and thus so interrelated with the psychic anatomy of each person—then indeed you have mastered the greatest secret of life and, on the basis of this understanding, you will be able to correctly analyze all human behaviorisms. You can rationalize any and all cases of various idiosyncrasies and vicissitudes of human nature.

Conversely, until such time as you do understand, you are your own worst enemy and any attempts which you might make either to analyze yourself or to correct any aberrations or malformations of the surface or daily life may well not only be fruitless but can be very dangerous and could lead to more complete solidification of these existing aberrations.

To review what has been explained to you, it is now easily understandable that man is the greatest enigma of all enigmas and this is especially true of all those who are the so-called practitioners and purveyors of human welfare, for none of them understand these principles even though they hold the power of life and death, holding it by virtue of the faith and trust their fellowman has placed in them—an unrequited faith and trust—and most usually climaxed in the familiar funeral procession trailing to the nearby cemetery. Even worse than this is the grave with the unmarked headstone which any person will dig for himself if he attempts to solve the enigma of his life from these outside sources.

In the foregoing text, we have definitely established certain precincts of knowledge which, up until this time, may have been quite unknown to you. However, they are provable, not only in the laboratories of our scientific world but they will be proven to you in the future as true in the countless thousands of lifetime experiences which, up until now, have only confused you more and bogged you down deeper into the mire of karma.

Now, as you begin to expand your consciousness with these principles, so likewise will lifetime experiences expand your knowledge of these principles and you will begin the actual recreation of the higher Spiritual Being which you will become if you include these principles in a more complete dimension of life.

It is indicated, however, that an even stronger junction of consciousness be established at this time with the principles contained in the foregoing context material. There is an old cliché which came out of the East, about the tail trying to wag the dog, and up until this point at least, you have, in a figurative sense, been as the tail trying to wag your dog. In other words, as has now been proven, the most important part of your life was going on in a way in which you were not conscious; you were still trying to control these unknown elements in the customary reactionary way.

You must remember that you cannot at any time attain reason by any mental effort until you have formed a junction as a functional process with all of these heretofore unknown elements. And though it may seem strange to you at the moment, in your future dispensations of life you will, whenever this complete junction is attained and so expressed as reason, become one of those Spiritual Beings who are frequently pictured or described as Masters.

It might also be well to note that at these specific times, whenever the perfect junction takes place, there will be no limitations of consciousness; there will be no reactionary interplay of emotions. You will be able to tune into the proper solution to any and all problems; your mind will function as a clairvoyant instrument and, in those golden moments, you will realize that there is no such thing as astral flight but, instead, you will conceive the new concept of attunement and function with all things simultaneously. You will not need to travel astrally, for the perfect image of what you seek is immediately attuned—a process which is somewhat like that which makes your television function and, as a matter of fact, you are at any and all times, functioning just as does the television set; except up until the present time, you have not been conscious of the transmitter or the studio from whence the pictures of your life came. Neither were you conscious of the method of transmission.

Here again is a very important point to remember: the very essence of learning and usage of these principles will depend, in the future, on just how well you can bring together these various principles of function. For, you will neither learn these principles nor practice the knowledge until such junctions are made and they begin to form various vital parts of your new psychic anatomy.

In the future, therefore, become conscious in all things that you do or that are manifest on your surface life, that these surface manifestations are like the ripples on the surface of a lake, caused by the reactionary processes of that which you formerly called thinking; that, by far, the greatest part of you is functioning in the great invisible worlds just beyond your sight or hearing.

Try to visualize thought as an oscillating motion, like the little green snake crawling through the grass. Visualize your subconscious as something like a large bucketful of live fishworms, all crawling in and out of each other, for these are the reactionary and sometimes unrelated past lifetime experiences all brought together, in fact, re-created by the ever resurgent frequency principle.

Quite naturally, you will begin to realize the importance of reconstructing your psychic anatomy from more suitable material, for it should not be constructed from the same age-old elements of fear, lust, greed, envy, and guilts. For, if you reconstruct your new psychic anatomy from such coercive elements, you will only have another bucket of fishworms.

Instead, try to be a sensible architect of your future. Begin the rebuilding process out of the logical reason and purpose of all things, thought, form and action. When you have found the logical reason, then you have found the purpose of the Infinite and, in finding all of these new elements, you will indeed begin to function as an architect, building for yourself not only a new and shining spiritual anatomy, but a home constructed of Radiant Energies and part of a community of advanced personalities in one of the higher planes of life. And, in occupying this new psychic or spiritual anatomy, you will take your place among the dwellers of the higher planes; for indeed you will have found your Nirvana, your Father Within and your Kingdom of Heaven—a more complete junction and function of consciousness with the Infinite.

*   *   *   *   *   *   *

A Moral Opiate

Karl Marx said, "Religion is the opiate of the people." The author quite agrees with this statement. However, the author also realizes that this religion (or code of ethics), plays an important part in any individual's life, whereby he discharges certain psychic pressures; a sort of leavening action which helps to prevent the accumulation of such static psychic pressures, thus preventing a common neurosis. It is doubtful that Karl Marx believed in, or understood reincarnation; neither did those individuals who are said to be at least partially responsible for the inclusion of Marxism in the Communist regime. It is easy to extract various elements into personal, conscious or subconscious configurations, thus giving rise to surface conformities which are not original in their content.

When any person looks into a mirror, he subconsciously tries to see himself as he wishes to be. This is a subconscious reactive principle which occurs in any

163

sequence of life experiences as they are expressed from day to day with any individual. This personal, subconscious, reactive remodeling is done with the express purpose of preventing possible ego deflations should large nonconformities occur, for these nonconformities present adverse and sometimes insurmountable mental objectivisms. The old cliché, "Love me, love my dog", is quite applicable here. Every person loves to be loved, for any display of attention from one person to another, must always justify not only the insatiable longing to be recognized, which exists in every individual, but that this person must be recognized for what he believes he is—which is often quite different from what he actually is.

Observations or the philosophical dogmas which are engendered from such surface manifestations of human conduct must always be purely compromises unless such philosophical observations can include more scientific aspects. Purpose and the reason for purpose, whether it is contained in an individual life or an individual expression, must include individualization of this purpose.

CHAPTER 26

The Great Hoax

It has been observed countless numbers of times that it takes all kinds of people to make a world; however, the full implications of this humble bit of philosophy are not fully realized except by those people who are interested in and are performing some humanitarian effort. This is particularly true when such an effort involves personal elements of a psychological nature and in which some such person, who may be attracted by this humanitarian effort, can see or read into it a possible means of escape from one or a host of sins, iniquities, derelictions and aberrations.

In this general escape mechanism, these escapists are attracted en masse to the standard of any such real or phony humanitarian efforts. Unfortunately, almost all efforts so tendered have, to a large degree, been of such phony or invalid characteristics; they have all promised, but failed to deliver. Perhaps the greatest single character in our modern times to capitalize on this human frailty was Phineas T. Barnum and his various fraudulent activities which are historically well-known.

However, other great frauds which have been perpetrated on humanity are not so generally recognized. In fact, the greatest of these has gone for thousands of years unrecognized, except by a very few, for what it really is—a great hoax. This great hoax is religion and in general classifications of all religion, past or present, the present-day Christian orthodoxy—or whatever it is called—is the greatest single representation of this great fraud.

We may attempt to justify or rationalize the existence of these religious systems. We may say that they were necessitated as a general development in the mental and spiritual qualities of mankind throughout the ages. However, this optimistic philosophy is soon dissipated when we strip religion bare of its veil of mysticism and present the bare, ugly machination behind religious systems.

In common, all religions had a similar basic starting point. They were first born in the primitive mind of the jungle savage as he watched bolts of lightning crash from the stormy skies, or that he saw a great volcano spewing forth its lava. These and countless other natural phenomena gave rise in the savage mind to a system of justifications. These unknown mystical potentials were given personal identification and a symbolic pantheology was built around them.

Today, Christianity still clings to these vicious symbologies. It has built around them its own pantheology, adding strength to this viciousness; for under its stifling cloak, reason and self-initiative are snuffed out and every person who so believes in this system is strangled by the cord of salvation, held in the hands of his fancied "savior". Yes, the common escape mechanism, engendered by fears of want, insecurity, greed and lust, have made helpless slaves of any and all of those who are attracted into the mesmeric mists of these false hinterlands, led there by the bloody cross and equally bloodied robes of those who carry it.

The crucifixion should become a symbol, not of salvation, but a symbol of personal crucifixion to any persons who follow this pagan symbology. There is only one way to attain this long-dreamed-of salvation;

166

that is, to take the pathway of constructive evolution and to gain the first foothold on this pathway; to take the first step means that every person who so starts must discard his ancient pagan symbologies. In their stead, he must rebuild and reconstruct an entirely new dimension of purpose and attainment; he must begin to attain certain scientific knowledge which makes the function of the Infinite Creative Intelligence possible.

This knowledge cannot be symbolized; neither is it reducible to some mathematical formula. It is more than knowledge. It must actually become the factual working elements and ingredients of each personal life. It mandates personal responsibility for every thought and action as part of the function of this Infinite Creation.

Unfortunately, the present mental horizon of any existing human being cannot encompass such broad extractions. All humans are living under a rote system; each action or reaction is some part of the various reactive and instigating forces which surround this human. Under these conditions he does not and cannot either sustain or originate constructive individual thought and action. Perhaps this statement may be very startling but careful analysis with any or all people yields the same results. They are all following these same reactionary patterns and rare indeed is the person who gives rise to some new and original thought and action which is beyond the dimension of his earth life.

If we look about us in our present times, we may see many new scientific inventions which may seem to be the result of some more highly developed creative effort by those responsible for them. However, here, too, analysis will show that these various inventions and developments have also been born as the progeny of some great necessity. Their parents may be great idealisms wedded to earthly fears and frustrations and, from these strange minglings, some creation is born.

So it was with the Wright Brothers and the first aircraft. Yet, Leonardo da Vinci, as well as countless others in bygone ages, longed for and visualized the free soaring flight of birds. This, too, was part of the great escape mechanism.

In general, therefore, all classifications of individual spontaneous reactive efforts of humans can be said to be engendered from some such an escape mechanism. A painter who puts beauty on a canvas is only temporarily escaping the vicissitudes of earth life in some subliminal self-creation and in a semi-cataleptic state, he ascends into the arboreal regions of some fancied realm when, in his transported condition, some of the beauty may leak off into the paint which he daubs upon the canvas. And, as with the artist, so it is with all those who seem to be creative, even including those who may be self-sufficient in their creative efforts.

We cannot deny the existence of great spiritual worlds beyond this third dimension; in fact, any form or substance, even in the existence of man himself, would be but a hollow mockery, a useless and unintelligent freak of happenstance unless there were such great worlds beyond this.

How natural then, for man in his earthly mire, to seek an escape from all the insecurities, sins and iniquities which are inherent to this plane. For, is not man born of this infinite substance? Like all things, large or small, the earth and all its creatures have been created from this sublime spiritual stuff.

Each thing, though it may appear to be different, is a highly developed and organized system of tiny solar systems of energy and these, in turn, claim as their parents, the very substance of the Infinite Mind. Yet, as of today, almost all mankind walks in ignorance of all this. His eyes are darkened against that which must reach through to him before he can escape from his self-constructed pit of clay, for while he clings to this cross or his heathen gods, he will be blind to his Kingdom of Heaven Within; for he will constantly re-create new ways, new means and new methods to justify his false symbologies.

No man is saved, save that he is reborn of the spirit; these words uttered 2000 years ago have the same meaning today, for within the countless creative effigies of the Great Intelligent Mind which lives within every human, yet he and he alone must seek and find them and only he will be so reborn when he finds them; for in the finding of these countless creative effigies, man finds the living of his own life in them and, in the living, so do these effigies become the new man and he is reborn again.

How well then that we, whoever and whatever place in life we may now occupy, let us see that wherever we are, each and all things about us are part of this great effigy of the Creative Mind. Let us see it not as some symbol or system of symbologies but as a definite, active, re-creative part of the Great Infinite Creative Mind. When we have formed, within our minds, this constant never-ending re-creative form and substance, then we can begin to fashion a new home for ourselves; not made from the reactive symbolic forms of these material worlds, but made from form and substance which is creative in nature and part of the Infinite Effigy.

So we will be born again, and of spirit; not by the words of false minions who, in their false deifications, are still perpetrating the great hoax and, in this creation, we will find that the very nature of the material world, each man's life is the greatest hoax of all; for in living this life, man seems bent upon every destructive purpose. He is wanton and wasteful with all the abundant resources which are part of his world. He will spend great wealth to kill his fellowman in some fancied deviation of life, or he is forced to spend his resources in defending himself from other false ideologies. He will erect great hospitals and use all his technical skill and knowledge to perpetuate a miserable life for hopelessly crippled people and use even greater technical skill and resources to decimate the world of its strongest youth. He will judge a man to die for the death of another, even though the power of his judgment is vested in him by a government guilty of mass murder.

And while he is doing these things and many more insoluble and perplexing mysteries, he is deifying himself and, in his eulogy, he claims kinship with the Creator. He will even go so far as to claim complete salvation from all his sins and iniquities by crying out the name of a man who tried to show him a better way 2000 years ago. And while we are pondering on these and many strange paradoxes of human nature, which can we rightfully say is the greatest hoax? For, even in the creation of these different hoaxes and in the living with them and by them, man has only betrayed himself; that he and he alone, individually or collectively, is the greatest of all hoaxes; and that he, Judas-like, is daily betraying himself for the few pieces of silver which represent his earthly life.

He betrays himself when he gives power to others over him, and when he assumes power over others he is also betrayed. And so life has been lived by man for thousands of years; each age and each civilization has brought forth its new hoaxes and even as of today, man is still living by them. They are the same as when man first found them in the jungles of long ago. They are the same as those lived and worshipped in the yesterdays and, as of each day and each time, man has dressed them in new garments and given them different names.

So it will be of tomorrow and those who are born in that future will find them again and they will clothe them differently and call them by new names. They will become the symbols in his place of worship; they will be the symbols in his monetary system. They will be heard in the screams and groans of the dying who have sacrificed their lives to them, for this is the way which all earth men take, and throughout this great universe and its countless galaxies and even more countless solar systems—many with worlds like our own—mankind is still following and finding his symbologies. He is still deceiving himself! He is still perpetrating the same reactionary system of hoaxes. This, he will do until his judgment day when he judges himself as his own betrayer and, in his prison in which he has cast himself, he will seek out the one small window through which the radiance of the inner light shines and, as he seeks the light, so is he purified and made whole; and in his wholeness, he is reborn and in the radiant beauty of his new spiritual body, he will fly like a homing dove to the higher worlds of Light.

CHAPTER 27

Believest Thou This

Throughout the course of written or unwritten histories of man's life upon the planet earth, there is no doubt that without exception, no single element has been of greater importance to him than his religion. This has been true in all past civilizations for, collectively or individually, whatever man's beliefs were, whether they were pagan, Christian, agnostic or atheistic, he has always been subconsciously and consciously aware of many mystical forces and elements which were moving about him. These and other factors of life always influenced his thinking and caused him concern, not only in respect to this present day by day life, but his future and especially the more ultimate destiny of some theoretical heaven.

In the pursuance of these various ideologies, mankind has, universally, been very unrealistic in creating and re-creating the various mystical effigies of gods and their various prerogatives in their functional activities which supposedly controlled the destinies of all men. These concepts have always been illusionary and without the necessary scientific proof of their existence. It is always amazing to see people who are usually quite intelligent in their daily life and in their respective activities become like wide-eyed children in their approach to the most vital and important facet of their life—their personal religion.

172

Throughout the ages they have been duped into countless unrealistic versions of religious aspects; they have been promised fantastic rewards consisting of health, healing and after-life salvation, to lead a further unrealistic and unhealthy existence of nothing more than complete idleness or with conditions tailored to the greatest, fanciful degree of opulent power. In these respects, present-day Christianity takes a foremost place among these various religious configurations which have duped the masses of humanity since their beginning and, in this present day, this great religious hoax is still flourishing despite great scientific knowledge which completely disproves the messianic content of its liturgy; for in the very foundation of this religion which is based primarily upon the life of Jesus, we find the written descriptions of the life of this man contain great distortions, obvious fabrications and much elimination of the true happenings which were so outstandingly expressed by this person.

Without a doubt, the greatest single and most outstanding proclivities of Jesus were his abilities to heal people; at least, if we believe the New Testament verbatim, we would, just as have countless other millions, be completely overawed by these stupendous miracles and healings. However, there are many Christians, principally a scientific element, who do not believe these miracles ever happened or believe that they were largely fables—falsely colored happenings, without fact or scientific background, and whether or not you do or do not believe in these miracles, it would be best as a seeker of truth, if you did scientifically analyze the descriptions of these miracles as they are written in the New Testament.

Here again, regarding the Bible itself, we are presented with that same obvious psychological quirk of human nature—for without knowledge, hundreds of millions of good people have swallowed hook, line

173

and sinker, practically the entire contents from cover to cover, the entire Bible. So far as the New Testament is concerned, however, we will begin first to understand its origin and how it was written.

None of the Apostles could read or write and so far as can be historically ascertained, no written record or diaries were kept. Furthermore it was not until 25 or 30 years after the crucifixion that any attempt was made to record these happenings.

Paul commissioned his two priests to start writing the New Testament which was done in Greece, many miles from the original site. These priests had to prepare these various gospels from any existing sources. They drew from the memories of those people who were still living and remembered certain incidents. They were also considerably influenced by other religions and by the necessity of impounding into these newly formed gospels, the necessary elements which would attract people by a mystical aura and they were also quite possibly influenced by their own somewhat fanatical, religious position. Also, further writings and rewritings occurred hundreds of years after the first versions, creating new distortions.

Analyzing the situation in these respects, we can easily see how the New Testament became falsely colored, distorted and otherwise fabricated. To further prove this point, let us analyze the very miracles themselves. The first dominant fact which asserts itself is the complete and total purposelessness of these miracles save a very lame excuse, which some people might interject, that these miracles were performed so that Jesus might establish His mission on earth, or He felt sorry for them—compassion is another popular excuse. However, we cannot ever hope to justify a miracle upon the premises in which they are presented to us in the New Testament. Neither can we justify them with any other logical reason or supposition and we will be forced to conclude that, even though Jesus was wise enough to work miracles, He did so in complete ignorance of several important psychological aspects, or that He did them illogically despite his knowledge of them were these Biblical depictions true—which they were not.

What are these psychological reasons? First, any person who has such a miracle performed for him has been very severely cheated out of his personal victory over this condition. Secondly, he has been cheated out of the knowledge to overcome this condition. Thirdly, he has been cheated out of any future usage of this knowledge which would either prevent an aberration or should one occur, he could then correct it. Fourth, he has been cheated out of the ability to teach and demonstrate to countless other people the correct acquisition and usage of knowledge which would enable these countless thousands to also learn this knowledge to correct their conditions and in turn they could teach others, ad infinitum. Therefore, we must conclude that there is much that could and should be added and subtracted to the new existing synoptic gospels if they are to cease being illusionary to countless millions of people who are presently concerned with them and to countless millions who may become enmeshed in the coils of these false portrayals.

No doubt Jesus did perform many great miracles and that in some respects they have partially entered into the New Testament. However, by no means could these be so justified unless we realize there were many unrecorded factors entering into these miracles; factors which were unknown and not understood by those who witnessed their happening. To you personally, however, there is a much greater implication in which you may become involved, if you accept the doctrine of miracles prima facie. You, like countless millions of other people, will likewise become enmeshed in the coils of false suppositions.

Your prayers for your own personal miracle will become only the outside manifestation of a deeply rooted subconscious escape mechanism, one which blinds you to the scientific reality of your progressive evolution, your ability to properly learn true cause and effect; the power which this wisdom will give you to overcome all conditions and to prevent any recurrences, for without exception, any and all conditions and diseases from which mankind is so presently suffering, all past, present and future conditions are completely soluble. They can be healed, not by an unrealistic miracle performed by some deity, but by the miracle of understanding and the proper usage of this knowledge and in the acquisition of this knowledge and wisdom from life to life; its correct usage in a direct proportion to your acquisition will always keep you tangibly related and situated to your evolutionary course and the Infinite Creator who is constantly living through you as you so acquire it in this manner.

*The truth regarding the miracles is told in "The True Life of Jesus" book—an amazing revelation.

CHAPTER 28

The Kingdom Within

It has been universally observed that the Bible is the most contradictory book ever written. This is quite true, for within the historical framework of this book, we find all known elements which relate to human conscious or subconscious behaviorisms and the beliefs which sponsor these various human reflexes.

Within the Bible there is found, mingled together, fact and fiction, history, superstition; and love is found side by side with murder. Altruistic idealisms are affronted in close proximity with fornication, conniving, lustful purposes and over all there is a glossed coating of supernatural aura contrived as a buildup of preconditioning by all those who associate their life with the Bible. It is difficult indeed to reconcile or compromise a god who would slay 20,000 Israelites worshipping a golden calf, with the god of Jesus who taught and expressed the most benign and beneficent attitudes, to turn the other cheek, as told. Yes, even this God has been vilified; for even in the very act of procreation, as the Father of Jesus, he was guilty of adultery or that his representative priest performed this adulterous act for him.

Attempts to separate the two dimensions of the Old and New Testaments only defeat the validity of any and all spiritual values which it may contain and any person with an ounce of brains and the ability to use them, would discard the whole book so far as its moral influence was concerned and regard it as it should be regarded—a historical compilation of fact and fiction—and leave it up to those who fanatically mesmerize themselves into believing its contents as a way and means of their own personal salvation.

This presents a great mockery and a great hypocrisy. Those countless millions of poor souls, past, present and future who have, or will become so mesmerized and accept this book verbatim as a way of life, have found or will find the hollow mockery of this miasmic mysticism. They will wander through the ages, living life after life, yes, living death after death; suffering untold tortures in their self-inflicted purgatories until they learn to discard the influence of this book and the ecclesiastical systems which it has fostered and supports.

Yes, even the words of its greatest single character, Jesus, have been mocked and from them there has been compounded the greatest of all hypocrisies which lives and enslaves the untold millions who believe in and express this hypocrisy.

And yet, far worse and more far-reaching are the damnable effects of this false hypocrisy, when the expressionists attempt to carry it into the far corners of the world and enslave other countless millions; for in this traumatic fanaticism, none of these believers and expressionists can rest or sleep as long as there is a single living soul who is not fanatically mesmerized, as they are. And so with their Bible and cross, they have pushed themselves into the palaces of kings and the huts of beggars; they have ridden camels and donkeys, walked the continents shod or bare-footed in the insatiable desire to convert all mankind to their false ideology.

The existence of God is never denied; yet this God must never become a personal entity endowed with

various human frailties, vicissitudes and tempera-
ments; instead, within the dimension of your personal
life, your God should be the Infinite, Creative Intelligence which has created and is a part of all things.

Instead of trying to form your own course of action
along the pathway of life and evolution, from the torn,
twisted and distorted fragments of fact and fiction
which exist in the Bible and which have been further
torn, twisted and distorted by those self-deified religious expressionists, begin to learn of the true Infinite
Creator in your daily life. Through the doorway of
your mind, will come a great flood of creative information; you will begin to see the plan, purpose and
expression of the Creative Intelligence in all things.

These will be your first steps into the Kingdom of
Heaven Within; a message and principle from Jesus
which has been so vilified in the ecclesiastical systems and expressions which have completely exploit-
ed and capitalized upon all human frailties and weaknesses and which have been expressing their own
particular hypocrisy even in contradiction to other
hypocrites.

Jesus taught one simple principle, self-emancipa-
tion, which every individual attains when he begins to
learn of the Creative Intelligence in the dimension of
his own mind when he can connect his present existence with the past, present and future as it exists
in the timeless dimensions of Infinity; when he realizes that he is, even now, a star dweller, and that in
the future eons of this timeless, interdimensional
Infinity, he will wander from planet to planet, from
galaxy to galaxy, always attracted to these places by
the appearances of those things he can conceive and
believe in within his mind. This is his immortal
heritage, not given him through the eyes of another
person who cannot see as he does; for all things of
which a man is and does, are always products of his
own mind, as he relates his position to the infinite

prospectus.

"Seek and ye shall find; knock and the door shall be opened," were the simple philosophical utterances of Jesus; simple direct ways to attain all unknown dimensions of understanding wherein could be found the true solution to all enigmas. How then can anyone hope to achieve immortal salvation or personal emancipation by reading a historical archive which was almost totally compounded by people caught in the tremendous forces and pressures of their own past worlds; people whose inner lives were nothing more than delirious fanatical dreams of their own past worlds, and whose daily lives were nothing more than unrealistic attitudes which found outward expression in psychotic mass subjugation in which the vilest and foulest demoniac expressions were given the sanction and sanctity of a false god.

For, if ye seek in these false archives such as the Bible, if ye seek through the doorway of a church or a temple, then you too will be equally vilified, even as those who have gone before. You will be diverted and perverted from attaining either the true cause and purpose of your existence or in freeing yourself from your present insecure, disease-ridden position; you will not find the true creation and its purpose by following the false doctrines compounded from the Bible.

For almost 2000 years it has been responsible, either directly or indirectly, for all of the wars, individual and mass murders, human misery and derelictions, self-deifications and crucifixions, sins, iniquity, perversions, adultery, complexes and a countless number of other degraded human expressions which have been done by those who have carried the Bible and the cross and who justified their actions, just as did the expressionists in the Bible—by the fancied sanctity of their false god.

CHAPTER 29

To See or Not To See

In the various epistles of Unarius, it has been frequently stressed that the doorway to heaven is not
found through some ecclesiastical system but rather,
by beginning to understand and by learning the functioning principles of the great Infinite Intelligence
through the doorway of personal consciousness. This
is quite true and the only way any person attains salvation from these material worlds. It is the way which
Jesus spoke of and pointed out to His people 2000
years ago.

Obviously, to begin to understand this Creative
Intelligence, we must begin at the bottom point in the
scale of evolution which is the material world. No
person could begin to understand the Creative Intelligence from the top, for he would have to be an Infinite Intelligence himself before such a feat could be
accomplished.

Paradoxically, most people go from cradle to the
grave without learning anything except a rudimentary
understanding of this great natural phenomena called
Infinite Intelligence. They have not bothered or desired to explore the cause and purpose of everyday Creative Intelligence going on about them every moment
of their lives; and in so concerning themselves with
the pressurized reactionary elements of their lives,
they have cheated themselves from obtaining the

knowledge and wisdom which is necessary for them to have before they can ascend to any spiritual domain. So far as can be ascertained, apparently most people who do aspire seem to have been literally forced into seeking the better way of life because of the mental and physical illnesses they incur in living a continual succession of karmic earth lives. For in becoming human, independent thought and action which is acquired in this humanizing process demands, as an equilibrium, that any person so beginning the acquisition of independent thought and action, must also learn correct usage, as well as the purpose, of this mental independence in the scale of infinite prospectus.

In order to better understand common abuses of this great opportunity of beginning to learn about the Infinite Intelligence, let us take a specific, everyday function which most people have and use in their daily life—namely sight. How many people are there who could be approached and give a clear definition of the phenomenon of sight? Not many; indeed even the more advanced scientist could give you only a partially inclusive and accurate description, for much of the process of seeing still lies outside the third dimension or physical dimension, not yet known or explored by science. For practical purposes, however, for an analysis we can confine our introspection within the known precincts of our third dimensional world. This will give us at least a starting point from which we can, at a later time as our consciousness expands, begin the inclusion of fourth dimensional aspects.

In looking at any particular object, you do not actually see this object; you are merely looking at the ends of a large number of tiny wave forms of energy which were reflected from that object. These pass through the lens of your eye which is so shaped that it bends or focuses them upon a tiny spot at the rear of your eyeball which is called the retina. This is a group of sensitive cells which contain phosphorous compounds and serve to change the wave lengths of these energies and send them on their way into the brain. However, one of the most interesting parts of this process is in the actual reflecting process which is taking place in the object we are seeing.

In the various texts of the lesson course, we have discussed the wonderful function of the psychic anatomy and how these wave forms of energy are so integrated as to reform tangible objectivisms. But at this time we shall confine ourselves to the other end, or the beginning of our seeing. Suppose we had a very powerful microscope which could magnify many hundreds of thousands of times. By using one of the lower powers, say about 100 thousand diameters, let us look at the surface of an object, say an apple. We have been looking at this apple in the customary way; we think it is red. Scientists do not know why we can see color. There are literally thousands of colors, yet all of these are only combinations of three basic primary colors: red, yellow and blue; and from these three are compounded a host of other colorations.

How is this done? First, we must understand that the sense of color is, like all other things of the material world—illusionary. There is really no color at all; we are only looking or sensing with our eyes in one or a number of wave lengths of energy. It is in these differences of frequencies, or the number of times they oscillate or fluctuate to us that we determine their color. This has been a concept you acquired in building your psychic anatomy over a period of many thousands of years in many hundreds of lifetimes. The various plant and animal species which inhabit the planet earth do not have the same facility of distinguishing colors that you have.

Some plants see or sense certain colors, (or wave lengths). The same is true with various species of birds, fishes and other forms of animal life. Therefore we can say that the development of color consciousness was a product of your evolution. This was partially accomplished through innumerable experiences in your earth lives. You polarized or became spiritually conscious of them in your spiritual lives in between lives. Thus, from life to life, there was a direct connotation of color consciousness which progressively developed as you developed other factors of integration which concern your earth life.

Getting back to our microscope and apple, let us look at the surface of the red apple with the power of 100,000 times magnification. Suddenly, we see, not a seemingly solid, hard, red surface, but lo, this has disappeared; instead, we see what apparently reminds us of a starry night sky. Scattered all about throughout our field of vision at widely separated points are oddly shaped clusters of tiny pinpoints of what look like small globes of brilliantly glowing fire. These clusters of glowing specks are what the scientist calls molecules. The smaller specks of light are atoms.

Now, let us increase our magnification to something like a million times. Suddenly, one of these small glowing specks seems to fill the complete area of our vision. Instead of being a speck of light, it resolves itself into a large number of even smaller specks of light. However, these are not stationary; they seem to be madly revolving about like the planets around the sun, each one following a circular path which looks like another cluster of light specks and which would be true as long as we can increase our magnification; we would find smaller and smaller solar systems. The small particles of light which we saw buzzing madly around each other is the electron of an atom; and each one too, is a solar system composed of other solar systems infinitely smaller and so on, ad infinitum. This is the world of the microcosm. All of these tiny light particles are following electromagnetic lines of force which are gyrating in the adjacent fourth dimension.

When we have gained a comprehensive picture of these molecules and atoms, let us look at another phenomenon which is occurring. These various bodies of energy stay very closely related to each other; that is, various groups of molecules would be very difficult to separate from these individual formations of molecules which are composed of atoms. We could not take a knife and cut them in two as we would an apple; we would have to take a great deal of energy and by using it a certain way, we could cause this molecule to fly apart or to recombine itself with other molecules. It would be much more difficult to separate an individual atom.

Scientists use great cyclotrons or betatrons to break atoms apart and require vast amounts of energy to split even one single atom. What is the force or power which holds atoms together in groups of molecules and what is the power which holds the atom together? This is the EMF, (electromagnetic field); a power which is radiated from the higher dimensions through various dimensions where it is re-transformed into various compatible frequencies to enable it to perform its function, and which is the controlling agent of all known and unknown third dimensional energy transpositions. This EMF is always found in any atom or molecule; in fact, it is the glue which holds them together. It is the power which is constructing and reconstructing the great invisible macrocosm.

However, so far as the atom is concerned, it again re-transforms itself into a third dimensional power which radiates from the atom in tremendously fast wave forms of energy. As these little wave forms of energy radiate out from the atom in a continuous and never-ending stream, they become that force or power in which is found the reactive component of all physical or material substances. These energies which stem from one kind of atoms may be entirely incompatible or foreign to other streams of energies radiating from another kind of atoms. This is what is called material reaction. The atoms in the human body are thus incompatible to the atoms of a steel automobile; thus an automobile can kill a human by crushing his body.

Other kinds of atoms may be compatible. The atoms which form molecules of water are very compatible to many other kinds of molecule combinations and enter in and mingle freely with them. However, in no case, except in atomic fusion, do atoms separate within themselves and recombine to re-form new kinds of atoms. This is because such function must take place in the fourth dimension which is the originating source of atoms; whereas, in the third or material dimensions atoms as combined in the form of molecules can mingle freely or be reactive to each other like groups of certain types of people who could mingle freely together, but might react against mingling with other types of people.

Now, this is the basis for understanding how you see the apple. Certain wave lengths of energy, which you call light, strike the surface molecules of the apple skin. Some of these energies may be compatible, in which case they mingle freely with the molecules and are not reflected; they are absorbed and you do not sense or see them. Other frequencies of light, however, strike the waves of energy which are radiating from the atoms. These collisions do not destroy the energies but cause them to bounce like a rubber ball against a wall; thus some of these light energies will be bounced away from the apple and you will intercept or see them. The apple appears to be red because the longer, or so-called red frequencies are bounced back; the (so-called) yellow and blue frequencies of wave lengths are absorbed, or mingle with the molecules and atoms of the apple skin. That is exactly how you see color.

So you see, in following the scientific analysis, you can look back upon your past life and see how the daily, minute by minute process of seeing is a very wonderful, complex manifestation of Infinite Intelligence, very scientifically integrated and immutably following the exact principles which this great Creative Intelligence has built into every function of the microcosm and the macrocosm.

A moments thought will clearly point the way to you; that life in the future will be a constant and continuous advancement according to how well you begin to learn these functioning principles. Conversely, if you do not learn of them, you will gradually begin to destroy yourself. The existence and expression of life in any form is predicated upon the principle of continuous and progressive evolution. Nothing is static, nothing is solid; all forms and substances visible or invisible, are constantly regenerating in this progressive cyclic evolution.

The only true way any person can advance into the higher spiritual worlds is through the doorway of understanding and up the pathway of progressive evolution.

CHAPTER 30

False Teachers and Prophets

Certain wise Avatars who have visited this planet have always stressed man's perversities in distorting spiritual virtues into some subversive malfunction to obtain power and glory over his fellowman. History reveals kings and emperors have thus been born and as of today they are still reappearing in different clothing and with different names.

Not the least of those who set themselves up in some position of power over mankind is the priest and just as are other forms so represented, the priest and his ecclesiastical dispensation is still an all-powerful influence in almost any land on the planet Earth. It is a fact almost beyond analysis that the masses of people who have so lived in their time have accepted without quibble any and all claims of those who proclaim a visitation from the pervading ruling god of the times.

And so, whether it was Moses and the burning bush, Mohammed, Joseph Smith or any other historical configurations, these claims have caused these believers to form a religion or cultistic pantheology which always becomes extremely rhetorical; in fact, it lives and thrives by a fanatical demand that all mankind must so believe.

Nor is this fanaticism always confined to religious beliefs. Today's cold war with Russia is a point in toto as a political example of man's proclivities to either individually or collectively bend all other men to his or their will—that they must obey and live by his creed.

Unfortunately for those who believe and follow some self-styled prophet or holy man, or politico, the claim to "divine" leadership is, and always has been, completely false. The claim of divine visitation, command and leadership has always been born out of the warped and distorted subconscious of this self-called prophet. He has created this god in the dungeon of his own mind; given it all of the various vicissitudes of his own character, then given it a false doctrine which, in application, creates a convenient escape hatch to all those weaklings who are gullible enough to swallow his story—those who have neither brains nor willpower to solve their own differences and problems in a realistic manner.

It was in this way that Paul destroyed the mission and purpose of Jesus. There are others, too, who followed after other teachers and created their own all-powerful effigy; the motivating power and purpose was to relieve the psychic pressures in their subconscious which were born of want and insecurity and their failure to adjust themselves to life.

Then, too, the strength of this false leadership is seldom the product of their own particular life, as it had developed in the course of their evolution which involved past lives and some somewhat similar characterizations; also other life associations born and re-lived always tend to collect and add strength to this self-styled expressionist. And, he is further aided and abetted by astral under-world entities, some of whom have lived there "even unto the time of Noah", as was quoted by Jesus.

And so, as of today, we find the world in a chaotic state of existence; one which will destroy mankind unless new constructive leadership is found and

189

which can solve all these extremely complex problems. Such leadership would indeed be difficult to
find; much less would man be prone to accept it. For
it would be predicated upon the individual responsibility of each person to assume a constructive pattern
of life; to accept his own moral responsibilities for
every thought and action without the convenient
escape hatch furnished by some fancied savior or
intercessors; that each person, collectively expressing
with all the masses of humanity a life of purpose and
moral development, tailored by a long-range comprehensive plan of future evolution into higher planes of
life where various expressionary forms of living were
constantly expanding the mental horizons of these
people.

A moments thought reveals the tremendous change
which would have to occur in the thoughts and habit
patterns of mankind as he so lives. It would mean
a complete abandonment of all previous reactionary
elements motivated by the carnal and animalistic
instincts which are still being expressed by humans.
The lusts of hunger, sex, power, wealth, dominion, are
all inherent to mankind either as of yesterday, today,
or tomorrow as necessary adjutants in his struggle
for survival upon a material planet which sponsored
his very beginnings.

It would also mean destruction of his religious
effigy; he could not further depend upon the moral
opiate of religious salvation, he would have to destroy
other ideologies and systems and re-create, in his own
mind, an entirely new concept of life based upon the
great creative principle which Jesus called the Kingdom of Heaven Within.

Each man would also have to destroy the illusion
of mass which compounds his material world and
replace it with a functional science of interdimensional re-creation. These and many more elements of
earthly life would have to go "down the drain" before

man could follow leadership which could lead him out of this present-day chaos.

Obviously, no person could make these tremendous changes, at least not in one lifetime. Nor would such a course of action be wise even if feasible or possible; neither would any Avatar capable of such leadership be unwise enough to attempt it. To any advanced personality who has so attained a higher way of life, there is always a wise jurisprudence which gives this individual a correct knowledge of the function of various dimensions and their attendant modes of expression which are characteristically lived in various planetary systems and their attendant forms of life.

This advanced personality knows that man, as an evolutionary creature, is expressing a direct creative continuity into his earth life and thus begins to build the Supreme Creative Effigy within the dimension of his own mind and his attendant life expression. This is the ultimate way in which this Infinite Creative Intelligence becomes a personalized expression of Infinity, again re-expressing the creative function in all things, for it is conceivable that any man can attain this growth and expression.

Therefore the Avatar would not be so unwise as to try to change all men; he knows that any changes which occur within any person must be born from his own individual desire. He knows also, that this desire for a change and a better life is the result of personal quickening or preconditioning which occurs in the life lived in between lives or in earth life realizations. Then and only then can any person be helped.

Even so, again a wise jurisprudence must be maintained; a delicate equilibrium must be established whereby this person can always progressively maintain his development. At times he must be helped; he must also have suitable demonstrations to help keep his desire alive; but always must help be given in such a manner and quantity that he does not learn to depend upon it. The past has held for him a religious belief which taught dependency upon the self-styled purveyors of salvation; so a double problem must be overcome—absolution from the past, rebuilding a future from a host of unknown elements and always must he be aware to be ever alert, to constantly analyze thought and action completely, impersonally and objectively.

By now it is quite evident that collectively man cannot be saved; neither will he be destroyed on his planet Earth, for this planet is indeed a creation of Infinite Intelligence, conceived as a place whereby man could start a progressive evolution. To destroy either or both man or planet would destroy the plan and purpose of at least this small segment of Infinite Expression.

Yet, small as it is compared to the vastness of Infinity and its infinite forms, even such small destruction is inconceivable. Beyond and behind this seeming chaos and destructive trend, this Infinite Creative Intelligence is at work. It is functioning in an immutable way, far beyond the dimensions of human knowledge. And in this function, man will survive; this age will pass into another and a great cycle will have been concluded, just as others have been so expressed in countless past ages, each with its systems, its religions, its creeds and dogmas.

Yes, this too, is the future, for as man lives his evolution, so he comes and goes upon this and other planets, each time seeking an environment he can understand and live in and each time he adds to his knowledge of the Infinite. We who are wise in the ways of evolution, we who know of the plan and purpose, can only add some small part to your understanding; a part which is compatible to the way in which you interpret your present life. Nor can we exceed the limited dimension of your earth life, for to do so would only add more confusion to that which is already rampant in the world about you.

But do not despair, for even as the earth has so fostered its many ideologies and expressions, so there are countless other worlds, each with its own expressionary forms of life and, as a human, you possess the power of selection and discrimination which is above and beyond the circumstances of your environment. And if these words can be so conceived and are held fast within the vision of your inner eye, so will these worlds be achieved; each achievement a product of your dedication, your desire and your ability of conception.

Eternally Yours

Last night upon a garden path
  I walked with Christ
Yet this was not a tall and bearded
  man of faith I saw
But deep within I saw another form
  and molded in the form
Of what I am and even from the stuff
  of which I'm made
And deep within this form
  there glowed a radiance bright
Which came from out
  a great and Infinite Eye
This Radiance thought and spoke
  in soft and unheard, unknowns
  tongues
Of life eternal in some great Cosmic
  world the many things I'd learn
  about this life
In lives which I would someday live
So as this soft and Radiant Voice
  then spoke its message of Eternal Life
My garden path
  became a wondrous thing
Stretched out it was until its end
Was merged together with the stars

The Unariun Moderator,
Ernest L. Norman.